Cooking with

Days of our Lives

Ken Corday is executive producer of Days of our Lives. *His father, Ted, co-created the show and his mother, Betty, ran it until her retirement in 1985. The initial episode of* Days *aired on NBC November 8, 1965.*

Cooking with Days of our Lives

PAULETTE COHN *and*
DOTTY GRIFFITH
with Greg Meng

RUTLEDGE HILL PRESS

Nashville, Tennessee

Days of our Lives is presented by Corday Productions, Inc. in association with Columbia Pictures Television. Columbia Pictures Television is a SONY PICTURES ENTERTAINMENT Company.

Photographic credits: Photographs on pages 46, 135 *(right)* by Eddie Garcia. Photographs on pages 41, 65, 67, 73, 87, 88, 91, 92, 93, 96, 151 by Kathy Hutchins/Hutchins Photo. Photographs on pages 77, 155 by Jeff Katz/Jeff Katz Photography. Photographs on pages 26, 53, 61, 64, 121, 131, 146, 173 by National Broadcasting Company, Inc./Dave Bjerke. Photographs on pages 16, 20, 70, 109, 161, 164, 169 by National Broadcasting Company, Inc./Paul Drinkwater. Photographs on pages 143, 157 by National Broadcasting Company, Inc./Chris Haston. Photographs on pages 22, 110, 111, 115, 136 by National Broadcasting Company, Inc./Gary Null. Photograph on page 34 by National Broadcasting Company, Inc. Photographs on pages 13, 15, 19, 21, 25, 28, 31, 37, 38, 43, 45, 47, 48, 55, 58, 60, 62, 71, 75, 81, 83, 84, 86, 97, 102, 103, 104, 106, 107, 119, 120, 124, 125, 126, 130, 134, 135 (left), 135 (center), 138, 139, 142, 144, 145, 149, 150, 154, 156, 158, 159, 160, 162, 165, 167, 171, 172, 175, 177, 179 by John Paschal/JPI. Photographs on pages 39 *(right),* 141 by Robert Sebree. Photographs on pages 147, 153, 174 by Columbia TriStar International Television/Gerald Weinman. Photograph on page 39 *(left)* by Dick Zimmerman.

Published in Nashville, Tennessee, by Rutledge Hill Press,
211 Seventh Avenue North, Nashville, Tennessee 37219.

Distributed in Canada by H. B. Fenn & Company, Ltd.,
34 Nixon Road, Bolton, Ontario L7E 1W2.
Distributed in Australia by The Five Mile Press Pty. Ltd.,
22 Summit Road, Noble Park, Victoria 3174.
Distributed in New Zealand by Tandem Press,
2 Rugby Road, Birkenhead, Auckland 10.
Distributed in the United Kingdom by Verulam Publishing, Ltd.,
152a Park Street Lane, Park Street, St. Albans, Hertfordshire AL2 2AU.

Cover and page design by Gore Studio, Inc.
Text layout and typesetting by Mark Foltz

Library of Congress Cataloging-in-Publication Data
Cohn, Paulette, 1948–
Cooking with days of our lives / Paulette Cohn and Dotty Griffith
p.   cm.
ISBN 1-55853-553-5 (hc)
1. Cookery.   2. Days of our lives (Television program)
I. Griffith, Dotty.   II. Title.
TX714.C573   1997   641.5—dc21 97-41552
CIP

Printed in the United States of America
1 2 3 4 5 6 7 8 9-00 99 98 97

ACKNOWLEDGMENTS

The authors would like to thank Greg Meng for his determination, vision, and guidance, without which this book would not exist; Lorraine Zenka for her moral support and the family album (if you had not gone first, we would still be doing research); Janet Spellman-Rider for storyline guidance; Prissy Shaffer for diligent recipe testing; Larry Stone and Mike Towle for their faith in this project; John Mitchell for good humor and a steady hand; and our friends and families for their patience and support during the production of this cookbook.

Contents

INTRODUCTION

Days of our Lives is as fresh and vital today as it was when it debuted on the NBC television network on November 8, 1965. One of America's most popular daytime dramas, *Days* has been the top-rated program among women ages eighteen to twenty-five since 1995 and the number one show among women eighteen to forty-nine since 1996—an enviable record, to be sure.

Days has achieved such stellar ratings by not being afraid to reinvent itself. Although the core families—the Hortons and the Bradys—have remained, bringing into the fold such other families as the Alamains, the Reeds, and the Blakes has enabled the show to explore an entire spectrum of fascinating stories involving love, obsession, betrayal, blackmail, and murder. Vivian Alamain, for instance, has taken part in many extraordinary adventures—from burying Carly Manning alive to escaping from the Pine Haven sanitarium in a blaze of glory by rescuing Laura Horton from a fire. She also has had an entire series of escapades with the evil Stefano DiMera that has caused problems for many residents of the midwest metropolis of Salem.

The diabolical DiMera has put John Black and his beloved Marlena Evans through some nightmarish times—Maison Blanche, the Queen of the Night and Paris schemes, and touting Susan Banks as a surrogate mother for Kristen Blake. John has had to cope with the secrets of his forgotten past, among them the discovery that he had been a priest, which occurred just in time to save Marlena from Satan's clutches.

Sami Brady Reed is a world-class schemer whose exploits are also highly memorable: drugging man-of-her-dreams Austin Reed, returning to Salem pregnant and stopping her sister's wedding, and feigning amnesia while plotting malevolent mischief. Austin's marriage to Carrie Brady was Sami's payback, but there is little doubt that she'll hatch another grand scheme. And Carrie's rushed wedding to Austin, accomplished after the couple had been forced to spend so much time apart, will undoubtedly lead to problems—especially since Carrie has developed feelings for Mike Horton. There are definitely unresolved issues in Carrie's life, the kind that make for great stories.

Bo Brady, his former wife and true love Hope Williams Brady, and his current spouse, the former Billie Reed, also have endured an incredible emotional journey. Just as Bo was pulling his life back together after Hope's presumed death and had learned to love again, Gina—a Hope look-alike with amnesia— turned up at the DiMera mansion in New Orleans. With Stefano involved, no one knew what to believe, but Gina came to Salem and ultimately vied with Billie for Bo's affections. Bo and Billie eventually were wed, but the marriage was invalidated when Gina regained her memory and it was revealed that she was in fact Hope. Billie sacrificed her happiness and left town to enable Bo to decide which of his two loves to pursue, but she returned and Bo later was forced to marry her in Rome. Bo owes Billie a tremendous debt for saving the lives of Hope and son Shawn-Douglas, and for helping him bring down drug lord JL King, but will he leave her to pursue Hope? Especially since Hope has vowed to move on with her life and may not be there for Bo.

Life has also been very trying for Jack Deveraux and Jennifer Horton Deveraux Blake. She thought she was a widow but is now convinced she needs to divorce a man the law considers to be dead. Peter Blake's obsession with Jennifer caused him to go along with Stefano's plan to frame Jack for a murder that never occurred. At Jack's re-trial, both Stefano and Kristen DiMera perjured themselves to keep Jack behind bars. Stefano wants to make sure that Travis Malloy, who has moved next door to Jennifer and is using the assumed name of Trent, can keep a watchful eye on Peter's wife. The dastardly DiMera is determined to help Peter recapture his lady love once Peter has healed sufficiently to get back into action.

With all the trials and tribulations of life in Salem, the only sure thing, besides death and taxes, is that our heroes, heroines, vamps, vixens, and villains will always find time to break bread. Cooking with *Days of our Lives* offers a delightful array of sumptuous cuisine enjoyed by your favorite daytime couples and singles—from breakfast in bed and intimate dinners for two to special celebrations, wedding feasts, holiday fare, quick and tasty meals for those on the go, and sinfully sweet confections. Share the romance of John and Marlena's breakfast à deux. Enjoy the intriguing international flavor of Bo and Billie's, Sami and Austin's, and Bo and Hope's nuptials. Explore Salem's hottest dining spots, from the elegant Penthouse Grill to the blue-collar Cheatin' Heart to the friendly Brady Pub. Join Shawn and Caroline for a classic Brady family Thanksgiving dinner, take part in the Horton clan's annual Christmas tree decorating party, and gather with both families and their friends for a festive summer picnic. Take a look behind the scenes at the delicious catered fare served to the cast and crew when taping of the show extends late into the night. Whatever the occasion, you're sure to find a host of mouth-watering menus and individual recipes that are sure to please one and all in *Cooking with Days of our Lives*. Try the recipes presented on the following pages—your taste buds and your loved ones will thank you!

Cooking with

Days of our Lives

1. COOKING FOR ROMANCE

*T*he mood is light and the time is right for making whoopee! As disparate as John Black, Bo Brady, Austin Reed, and Jack Deveraux are, they do have one thing in common: They definitely know how to get their respective ladies in the mood. Soft lights, candles, and beautiful music are just the beginning; these men know it also takes tenderness, consideration, a sense of humor, and often the element of surprise. This fabulous foursome knows that the sexiest thing about a man is his imagination, and each uses his in delightfully playful ways. For example, there was the night Bo pretended to be asleep in the bath on his boat, the Fancy Face, and pulled an unsuspecting—and fully clothed—Billie Reed in with him. You can guess what happened next. Then there was the night Carrie Brady came home to find her apartment looking like a florist's shop, with rose petals leading to the bedroom and Austin waiting at the end of the trail. They both woke up smiling the next morning. If you're looking for a recipe guaranteed to make the evening a smashing success, try one of these from Salem's scintillating sweethearts.

JOHN AND MARLENA: BREAKFAST IN BED

The qualities that make John Black such an incredibly sexy, tantalizing man are greatly enhanced by his total faith in his enamorata Marlena Evans, his thoughtfulness, and his tender gestures. John invariably brings home flowers and jewelry—and having inherited a portion of the Alamain fortune, he can well afford to do so. But what truly wins Marlena's heart are the gifts that don't cost money: loving, thoughtful deeds. John likes to surprise Marlena by making an intimate breakfast and serving it to her on an elegant tray in bed. When he knows Marlena is craving to spend time with the kids, John will sneak Brady and Belle into the kitchen to watch while he whips up a batch of pancakes for a special family breakfast. John's solicitous behavior isn't a once-a-year occurence like Mother's Day; it's the way he shows his love and devotion to Marlena day in and day out. What woman could resist?

MENU

STRAWBERRIES AND SHERRIED CREAM

LEMON POPPYSEED MUFFINS WITH BLUEBERRY BUTTER

HAM AND EGG CHEDDAR MUFFINS WITH MAPLE BUTTER

CHEESE BLINTZES

Strawberries and sherried cream

1   pint strawberries
1   cup heavy cream
1   tablespoon dry sherry or to taste
2   tablespoons confectioners' sugar

- Select large, perfect strawberries, preferably ones with fresh, unblemished green tops. They're prettier. Rinse the strawberries just before serving. Drain and gently dry with paper towels.

- Pour the cream into a small bowl and beat on high speed with electric beaters. When the cream begins to thicken, gradually add the sherry and sugar, beating continuously. Beat until the cream holds stiff peaks.

- Serve the strawberries on a silver tray. Place the sherried cream in a crystal bowl. Dip the strawberries in the cream and nibble. Better yet, give your partner a nibble.

MAKES 2-4 SERVINGS

Lemon poppyseed muffins

$^1/_2$ cup vegetable shortening
$^1/_2$ cup sugar
2   eggs, separated
1   cup all-purpose flour
1   teaspoon baking powder
$^1/_2$ teaspoon salt
$^1/_4$ cup lemon juice
1   teaspoon grated lemon rind
2   teaspoons poppy seeds

- Preheat the oven to 375°. Line mini-muffin tins with paper liners or spray with vegetable cooking spray.

- In a medium bowl, beat together the shortening and sugar until smooth. Add the egg yolks and beat until light and fluffy.

- Sift together the flour, baking powder, and salt. Add to the batter alternately with the lemon juice.

- In a small bowl, beat the egg whites until stiff. Fold the egg whites, lemon rind, and poppy seeds into the batter. Spoon the batter into the prepared muffin tins. Bake for 12 to 15 minutes or until golden. Serve with Blueberry Butter (recipe follows).

MAKES ABOUT 20 MINI-MUFFINS.

Blueberry butter

$^1/_2$ stick butter, softened to room temperature
1   tablespoon blueberry jam

- Place the butter and jam in the work bowl of a food processor or a blender container. Process just until blended. Place the butter-jam mixture in a ramekin or custard cup and refrigerate until ready to serve. Unmold and serve.

MAKES $^1/_4$ CUP.

Ham and egg Cheddar muffins

$^1/_2$ cup chopped ham
2   eggs, well-beaten, divided
1   cup all-purpose flour, sifted before measuring
2   teaspoons baking powder
$^1/_4$ teaspoon salt
2   tablespoons sugar
$^1/_2$ cup milk
2   tablespoons melted butter
$^1/_2$ cup grated Cheddar cheese

- Preheat the oven to 425°. Line mini-muffin tins with paper liners or spray with vegetable cooking spray.

- Place the ham in a small skillet over medium heat. Cook just until the edges turn brown. Pour in 1 well-beaten egg. Stir and cook until the egg is set. Remove from heat and turn out of the pan to stop the cooking. Allow to cool slightly, then chop or crumble the eggs to separate into pieces for folding into the batter; reserve.

- Sift together the flour, baking powder, salt, and sugar in a medium bowl. Combine 1 well-beaten egg with the milk and stir into the dry ingredients. Stir in the melted butter.

- Fold in the cheese and scrambled eggs. Spoon the batter into the prepared muffin tins. Bake for 15 to 18 minutes or just until brown on top. Serve with Maple Butter (recipe follows).

MAKES 12 MINI-MUFFINS.

JOHN BLACK

When he first appeared in Salem in 1985, he was swathed in bandages like a mummy and took the name John Black from a plaque on a soup kitchen wall. Everyone thought he was the "Pawn," but just as he was about to fall to his death from a cliff, Bo Brady concluded that John was really Roman Brady, whose appearance had been altered by plastic surgery. His memories were intact, and "Roman II" lived for several years as husband, "widower," and husband once again to Marlena and father to Carrie, Sami, and Eric. But when the real Roman returned, Roman II again became John Black—but not for long. First he was thought to be John Stevens and then the international jewel thief Romulus. But in the end, he turned out to be Forrest Alamain, brother to Lawrence and nephew to Vivian, who was forced to return a fortune she had swindled from Forrest. Because of his problems with the Alamains, and because it felt right, Forrest kept the name John Black. While trying to unlock the secrets of his past, John discovered that he had been a priest who was kidnapped by Stefano DiMera (even the vile Stefano couldn't bring himself to kill a man of the cloth), and had his memories erased and replaced with Roman's. John regained his faith in the nick of time to save Marlena from her possession by the devil. In return, Marlena saved John from marrying Kristen Blake DiMera, Stefano's stepdaughter, who proved to be every inch a diabolical DiMera. Just when it appeared that John and Marlena were finally going to reunite, Roman returned and stopped the wedding.

Maple butter

½   stick butter, softened to room temperature
1   tablespoon maple syrup

- Place the butter and syrup in the work bowl of a food processor or a blender container. Process just until blended. Place the butter-syrup mixture in a ramekin or custard cup and refrigerate until ready to serve. Unmold and serve.

MAKES ¼ CUP.

Cheese blintzes

1   egg, well-beaten
½   cup milk
¼   teaspoon salt
½   cup all-purpose or instant-blend flour
1   tablespoon butter, melted
Butter as needed for coating pan
Cheese Filling (recipe follows)
½   tablespoon vegetable oil plus ½ tablespoon butter
Confectioners' sugar
Fresh raspberries, blueberries, blackberries, or
    strawberries (optional)

- In a blender container (or small bowl), process (or beat well) the egg, milk, salt, flour, and butter. Cover and let stand for 30 minutes (unrefrigerated) or overnight in the refrigerator.

- Heat a 7- or 5-inch skillet or crepe pan over medium-high heat for 2 to 3 minutes, until hot. Remove from heat and brush a thin layer of butter on the bottom and sides. Use a pastry brush or a folded paper towel to apply the butter. The butter should very lightly coat the cooking surface of the pan. Pour off any excess.

- Pour about 3 tablespoons batter into the pan, quickly tilting the pan so the batter spreads evenly in the thinnest possible layer. Swirl and tilt the pan to spread batter in an even circle on the bottom and as far up the sides as possible.

- Cook until the bottom is light brown, edges lift easily from the pan, and the pancake slides easily. Remove to a plate. Repeat the process, coating the pan lightly with butter before cooking each crepe, until all batter is used.

- Place about 2 tablespoons Cheese Filling in the center of each crepe. Roll the crepe around the filling like an enchilada, seam-side down. At this point, the blintzes may be covered and refrigerated for several hours.

- When ready to finish cooking, heat the vegetable oil and butter in a large skillet over medium heat. Place several blintzes in the pan, seam-side down. Cook until golden brown, turning once. Repeat, adding more oil and butter in equal amounts as needed until all the blintzes are cooked.

- Sprinkle with confectioners' sugar and garnish with fresh berries, if desired. Serve with maple syrup.

MAKES 10 TO 12 BLINTZES.

Cheese filling

¾   cup small-curd cottage cheese
1   egg yolk
1   teaspoon butter, softened to room temperature
½   teaspoon vanilla extract

- Drain the cottage cheese. Blend the drained cottage cheese with the egg yolk, butter, and vanilla.

MAKES ¾ CUP FILLING.

BO AND HOPE'S TROPICAL DINNER

It was a warm summer night and the stage was set. Moored in the Salem River, Bo Brady's boat, the *Fancy Face*, was decked out with palm fronds, paper lanterns, coconuts, brightly colored fabrics, and grass mats. Framed by the lights of the town, wife Hope, in the persona of "Gina," appeared from belowdecks, wrapped in a sarong—just as she had done on that night so long ago. Bo, also dressed for the occasion, wondered whether recreating the special evening he and Hope had shared on their round-the-world journey would help her regain her memory, or only elicit thoughts put there when she was brainwashed by Stefano DiMera. In his quest for the truth about his former bride and mother of his child, Bo put all of his energies into making the night a success. The stakes were high as the lives of four people—Bo, Hope, son Shawn-Douglas, and Billie Reed—all depended on the outcome. The couple slipped into the water, and when Gina's sarong came off and began to float away, it kindled a spark of recollection in her mind. Bo came to her rescue, just like he did before, but they did not make love as they were still plagued by uncertainty. One thing that is certain, however, is that the following menu will have you yearning to experience the tropics' exotic ports of call for yourself.

MENU

SESAME SHRIMP AND SCALLOPS ON SKEWERS

TROPICAL THAI RICE WITH PEANUT SAUCE

GRILLED MAHI MAHI WITH ROASTED PINEAPPLE SALSA

COCONUT FLOATING ISLANDS

Sesame shrimp and scallops on skewers

4	large shrimp and 4 large scallops
2	wooden skewers, soaked in water
1	tablespoon soy sauce
1	tablespoon lemon juice
1	tablespoon oriental sesame oil
1/2	teaspoon finely chopped or shredded fresh ginger
2	teaspoons sesame seeds

- Prepare the grill or heat the oven broiler. When the coals are covered with gray ash, the fire is ready. If cooking under the broiler, lightly spray a baking sheet with vegetable cooking spray.

- Peel the shrimp but leave tails on, if possible. Thread the shrimp and scallops onto the wooden skewers, alternating them.

- In a small bowl, stir together the soy sauce, lemon juice, oil, and ginger. Brush the mixture over the skewered shrimp and scallops, coating all sides. Sprinkle evenly with the sesame seeds.

- Grill or broil the skewers 4 to 5 inches from the heat until the shellfish just barely turn white and firm up, about 3 to 4 minutes per side. Serve hot.

MAKES 2 SERVINGS.

Cooking for Romance

Tropical Thai rice

1 to 1 ¹/₄ cups water
¹/₂   cup long-grain rice
Peanut Sauce (recipe follows)
¹/₄   cup red pepper, cut in ¹/₄-inch cubes
¹/₄   cup unsweetened shredded coconut (optional)
¹/₂   cup honeydew melon, cut in ¹/₄-inch cubes
¹/₂   cup mango or papaya (or a combination), cut in
*   ¹/₄-inch cubes*
¹/₄   cup finely chopped fresh mint leaves for garnish

● Place the water and rice in a 1-quart microwave-safe dish. Cook on high for 4 minutes. Lower to 50 percent power and cook for 15 minutes, until the liquid is absorbed and the rice is tender. Remove from heat and allow to sit for 5 minutes. Transfer the rice to a large bowl and fluff with a fork to separate the grains and cool slightly.

● Stir in the Peanut Sauce. Add the red bell pepper, coconut, and fruit. Sprinkle chopped mint over the top. Serve barely warm or at room temperature.

MAKES 2 TO 3 SERVINGS.

HOPE WILLIAMS BRADY

It's a miracle that Hope turned out to be such a strong, independent, spontaneous, and fun-loving woman, considering the instability of her early life. She spent a very short time with her biological mother, Addie, who died saving Hope's life in a traffic accident. Then Hope was shuffled back and forth between Tom and Alice Horton (her grandparents) and Doug Williams (her father) and Julie Olson Banning Williams (her sister who later became Hope's stepmother). Otherwise, growing up as a Horton was a pretty good deal. In 1983, as a rebellious teenager, Hope was rescued from a drunken date by Roman Brady, for whom she immediately developed a crush. While babysitting Roman's twins, Hope met the true love of her life, Roman's younger brother Bo. Their relationship was a challenging one,
especially after Hope accepted a dare and became a cop. The romantic duo married in London and moved onto Bo's boat, the Fancy Face, which was his nickname for Hope. Following the birth of their son, Shawn-Douglas, Hope and Bo sailed around the world. After a series of adventures, including Bo's kidnapping by Ernesto Toscano, it appeared that Hope had died tragically in a vat of acid in Ernesto's hideout. Years later, she reappeared as "Gina" at Maison Blanche, Stefano DiMera's home in New Orleans. Bo moved on with his life and became involved with Billie Reed. Hope overcame all obstacles to prove her true identity and was finally reunited with Bo, only to have the relationship torn apart again. Despite knowing that Bo is the one great love of her life, Hope has vowed to move on.

Cooking for Romance

Peanut sauce

$^1/_3$ cup chicken broth
1   teaspoon finely chopped garlic
$^1/_4$ cup creamy peanut butter
1   tablespoon brown sugar
1   tablespoon soy sauce
1   tablespoon lemon juice
1   teaspoon finely shredded fresh ginger
2 to 3 drops red pepper sauce

● Combine the chicken broth and garlic in a small saucepan. Bring to a boil over high heat. Cook for 1 minute and remove from heat. Add the peanut butter, brown sugar, soy sauce, lemon juice, ginger, and red pepper sauce. Lower heat and cook, stirring constantly, just until the peanut butter melts and the sauce is smooth. Adjust seasoning to taste with lemon juice and red pepper sauce.

MAKES $^3/_4$ **CUP.**

Cooking for Romance

Grilled mahi mahi with roasted pineapple salsa

- ¹/₄ cup olive oil
- ¹/₃ cup fresh lime juice
- 1 tablespoon soy sauce
- 2 tablespoons finely chopped shallot or onion
- ¹/₄ teaspoon cayenne pepper
- 2 (6-ounce) mahi mahi (or other firm white fish) steaks, cut about 1-inch thick
- ¹/₄ teaspoon salt or to taste
- ¹/₄ teaspoon black pepper or to taste
- 2 tablespoons butter
- 2 teaspoons chopped cilantro for garnish

Lime wedges for garnish

Roasted Pineapple Salsa (recipe follows)

- In a resealable plastic bag, combine the olive oil, lime juice, soy sauce, shallot or onion, and cayenne pepper. Seal the bag and shake to combine. Add the fish steaks, reseal the bag, and turn to coat both sides. Place in the refrigerator for 30 minutes to 1 hour, turning occasionally.

- Prepare the grill or heat the oven broiler. When the coals are covered with gray ash, place the fish steaks on the grill. Cook for 4 to 5 minutes. Turn and grill for another 4 to 5 minutes. Do not overcook. The fish should feel firm, but not unyielding, when pressed in the center.

- Season the fish steaks on both sides with salt and pepper to taste. Place a tablespoon of butter on each to melt. Sprinkle cilantro over each steak. Serve with lime wedges and a dollop of Roasted Pineapple Salsa.

MAKES 2 SERVINGS.

Roasted pineapple salsa

1   fresh pineapple, peeled and cored
1   tablespoon freshly chopped cilantro
1   coarsely chopped serrano pepper (seeds and
         ribs removed)
2   tablespoons minced red bell pepper
1/4 teaspoon salt or to taste
1   teaspoon maple syrup

- Preheat the oven broiler. Cut the pineapple into 1/4-inch slices and arrange on a shallow baking sheet. Place under the broiler and broil until the edges are dark brown. Turn and broil the other side.

- Cut the roasted pineapple slices into large pieces and place them, along with any accumulated juices, in the work bowl of a food processor. Add the cilantro and serrano pepper. Process just until large pieces are broken up. Salsa should be chunky.

- Add the bell pepper, salt, and maple syrup. Refrigerate for up to 5 days.

MAKES ABOUT 1 CUP.

Coconut floating islands

1 1/4 cups milk
1/3 cup grated fresh or unsweetened flaked coconut
3   eggs, separated
3/4 cup sugar, divided
1   tablespoon dark rum or to taste
1   teaspoon vanilla extract

- In a medium skillet, combine the milk and coconut over low heat just until milk reaches a simmer. Adjust heat to maintain a simmer.

- Meanwhile, place the egg whites in a medium bowl. Using electric beaters, beat at high speed while slowly adding 1/4 cup sugar. Beat the egg whites until shiny and stiff. Using 2 soup spoons, scoop a spoonful of the meringue into one spoon, using the other to mound the meringue. Carefully slide meringue "island" into the barely simmering milk.

- Cook 3 meringues at a time for 1 to 2 minutes on each side or just until firm to the touch. Place on paper towels to drain while poaching the remaining egg white "islands." You should have 6 meringues. Remove the milk from heat.

- Place the egg yolks in a medium bowl and beat with electric beaters on medium speed until light in color and slightly thickened, slowly adding 1/2 cup sugar. Gradually add the warm coconut milk, stirring constantly.

- Pour the coconut custard mixture into a medium saucepan with a heavy bottom. Cook over low heat, stirring constantly, until the mixture thickens. Add the rum just as the mixture thickens. Do not allow to boil. Remove from heat and stir in the vanilla.

- Pour into a pretty cut-glass or crystal bowl and cool. Place a piece of waxed paper directly on the surface of the custard. When cool, arrange the islands on top. Chill well before serving.

MAKES 2 TO 3 SERVINGS.

CARRIE AND AUSTIN'S ROOFTOP DINNER

It was fate that led Austin Reed to move into the same building as Carrie Brady. Austin has long thought that Carrie is too good for him, but he's never denied that she brings out the best in him. Their special place—even though both are young executives on the move at Titan Industries—is on the roof of their building. They have spent many romantic evenings enjoying the sights of Salem from on high. The roof is where the star-crossed lovers were to meet on that fateful New Year's Eve when Sami changed the clocks and thus temporarily prevented Austin from reuniting with Carrie. But the roof also holds many positive memories for the pair, such as the night Austin set up a romantic tête-à-tête—complete with table for two, gleaming white tablecloth, silver candlesticks, Chinese lanterns blowing in the breeze, and love songs wafting from the portable stereo. The only thing missing was the perfect meal, which Austin ordered and had delivered, courtesy of Kate Roberts, from the Penthouse Grill. It pays to have a mother in high places.

MENU

Lobster bisque

Roasted pork tenderloin with brandied mushrooms

Rice pilaf

Wilted chard salad

Fresh lemon tart

Lobster bisque

1 (1 ¹/₂- to 2 ¹/₂-pound) live lobster
1   onion, quartered
1   carrot, cut in pieces
1   rib celery, cut in pieces
¹/₄ cup olive oil
4   cups water
1   cup heavy cream
1   tablespoon all-purpose flour
1   tablespoon butter, softened to room temperature
¹/₂ teaspoon salt or to taste
¹/₂ teaspoon white pepper or to taste
¹/₄ cup dry sherry or to taste

● With the tip of a large, sharp knife, quickly pierce the head of the lobster at the point on its back where the head joins the tail. This dispatches the lobster without any pain for the lobster and not much pain for the cook. But be careful! Grip the lobster firmly on a cutting board, using a towel or pot holder to prevent slipping. Then thrust knife point firmly and resolutely through the shell, all the way to the board. There, that's done. Breathe!

● If you choose, substitute two frozen lobster tails for the whole lobster. Roast according to the directions for live lobster.

● Preheat the oven to 450°. Place the lobster in a large, shallow roasting pan, front-side up. Using the knife tip, cut from the head through the abdomen so the lobster will lie flat with the meat exposed.

● Arrange the onion, carrot, and celery around the lobster in the roasting pan. Drizzle the vegetables and lobster with the olive oil. Place in the oven and roast, stirring the vegetables occasionally, until the lobster is bright red, about 20 minutes (10 to 12 minutes for tails). Meat should be white, no longer translucent. Avoid overcooking.

- Remove the lobster from the roasting pan and allow to cool enough to handle. Using crackers, crack the claws and remove the meat. Using a sharp knife and a fork, loosen the tail meat from the shell and remove; set aside, reserving the shells and the head.

- Meanwhile, return the vegetables to the oven and continue roasting until well-browned and easily pierced with a fork, 10 to 20 minutes longer.

- Remove the roasting pan from the oven. Return the shells and head to the roasting pan. Carefully pour water into the pan. Bring the liquid to a boil over high heat. Lower heat and allow liquid to simmer for 30 to 45 minutes or until reduced to about $2\frac{1}{2}$ to 3 cups. Stir occasionally to loosen bits which may be stuck to the bottom of the pan.

- When the liquid is reduced, carefully lift out the vegetables and shells with a slotted spoon and discard. Strain the liquid through a double thickness of cheesecloth into a clean saucepan and place over low heat.

- Chop the lobster tail and claw meat. Add to the stock and heat throughout. Add the cream. Heat throughout but do not boil. To thicken, blend the flour and butter to form a paste. Add the paste to the pot, stirring constantly, and cook until thickened. Add salt and white pepper to taste.

- Just before serving, add the sherry.

MAKES 4 SERVINGS.

CARRIE BRADY REED

Carrie is the eldest child of Roman Brady and the daughter of Anna Brady DiMera. But she was raised mainly by John Black (when he thought he was Roman) and Marlena Evans, and maintains a very close relationship with them. Carrie survived the normal problems of childhood as well as a broken arm sustained in a fall while ice skating and, more traumatically, being hit by a car. Unfortunately, Carrie didn't escape unscathed from Stefano DiMera's obsession with her family. When Carrie was only four, Anna hypnotized her as part of a DiMera plot to frame Roman. Later, Carrie was kidnapped and held hostage by Stefano. And there was a long period when she believed her father and stepmother were dead. But when Austin Reed came into her life, everything changed. Carrie fell in love with the handsome stranger, and nothing Roman said or did could discourage her. That is, until the night that Austin's shady past resulted in Carrie's face being burned by acid as the couple exited the party at which Carrie had been announced as the winner of Bella magazine's Face of the Nineties contest. That nasty bit of business kept the twosome apart for at least a year. Later, just when the reunited Carrie and Austin were to wed, Sami Brady broke up the ceremony by announcing that she was carrying Austin's baby. It's been a rocky period for Carrie, but she finally was able to marry the man of her dreams at the end of the summer 1997.

Roasted pork tenderloin with brandied mushrooms

1 or 2 (1½- to 2-pound) pork tenderloins
1   teaspoon salt or to taste
½   teaspoon black pepper or to taste
1   tablespoon Dijon mustard
About 1 tablespoon olive oil
1   teaspoon dried rosemary
1¼ cups beef stock, divided
2   cups sliced fresh mushrooms
2   tablespoons brandy or cognac
2   teaspoons cornstarch, dissolved in 2 to 3
       teaspoons water

- Preheat the oven to 350°. Rub the tenderloin with the salt, pepper, and mustard to coat all sides. Place a large ovenproof skillet over medium-high heat and add the olive oil. When the pan is hot, add the tenderloin, turning to brown all sides.

- Remove from heat. Combine the rosemary and ¼ cup beef stock. Pour over the tenderloin and place in oven. Roast for 30 to 40 minutes or until the pork is medium, with almost no pink remaining. It is not necessary to cook the pork until well-done. If desired, however, roast the pork up to 45 minutes for well-done.

- When the pork is cooked to the desired degree of doneness, remove the skillet from the oven and place the pork on a platter. Cover loosely with foil to keep warm.

- Place the skillet over medium heat and cook until most of the liquid is evaporated. Add the mushrooms and a bit more olive oil, if needed. Cook until the mushrooms wilt and begin to caramelize. Pour in 1 cup beef stock, stirring to scrape up any bits that may be stuck to the bottom of the pan. Cook over high heat until the liquid is reduced to about ¾ cup. Stir in the brandy or cognac and cook for another 1 to 2 minutes, just until the alcohol evaporates. Remove from heat. Stir in the dissolved cornstarch and return to low heat just to thicken.

- Add salt and pepper to taste. Slice the tenderloin thinly and serve with plenty of pan sauce and mushrooms.

MAKES 3 TO 4 SERVINGS.

Rice pilaf

To make a double batch, follow the directions in parentheses.

1   tablespoon olive oil
½   (1) cup chopped onion
1   (2) cup(s) long-grain rice
2   (3½) cups chicken stock
½   teaspoon salt or to taste
½   (¾) cup raisins, dark or golden

- Place the olive oil in a medium saucepan over medium-high heat. Add the onion and cook until soft, about 5 minutes. Add the rice, stirring to coat grains evenly. Cook for 2 to 3 minutes. Add the chicken stock and salt.

- Bring the stock to a boil and lower heat. Add the raisins, cover, and simmer until the rice is tender and the liquid is absorbed, 15 to 17 (17 to 20) minutes.

MAKES 4 (8) SERVINGS.

Cooking for Romance

Wilted chard salad

1   bunch red-leaf chard (about 2 to 3 cups leaves)
3   tablespoons olive oil
1   clove garlic, crushed
1   tablespoon red wine vinegar
1   teaspoon sugar or to taste
1/4   teaspoon salt or to taste
1/4   teaspoon pepper or to taste
1/2   cup Toasted Pine Nuts (recipe follows)

● Rinse and shake the chard dry. Remove large stems. Tear large leaves into bite-size pieces. Combine the olive oil and garlic in a large skillet over low heat. Cook for 3 to 4 minutes, stirring and mashing the garlic with the back of a spoon. Add the chard and toss gently. Cover the skillet and turn off heat. Set aside for about 5 minutes.

● Leaves should be wilted. If needed, raise heat for 2 to 3 minutes or just until the chard wilts. Sprinkle the red wine vinegar, sugar, salt, and pepper over the greens, tossing to evenly coat leaves. Leaves should be wilted but not cooked throughout. Sprinkle with Toasted Pine Nuts.

MAKES 2 SERVINGS.

Toasted pine nuts (pignoli)

1   cup pine nuts

● Place the pine nuts in a skillet over medium heat. Cook for about 3 minutes, tossing or stirring frequently to prevent burning.

● Remove the nuts from heat when edges start to brown. Continue to toss or turn a few minutes to stop the cooking.

MAKES 2 (¹/₂-CUP) SERVINGS.

Fresh lemon tart

4   *lemons*
2¹/₃ *cups sugar, divided*
Crusts for 2-crust pie (see Simple Pastry recipe
        on page 58)
6   *eggs, divided*
1   *tablespoon water*

● Cut off the ends of the lemons. Slice the lemons paper thin and remove the seeds. In a large bowl, combine the lemon slices with 2 cups sugar and toss to coat the slices evenly with sugar. Cover the bowl and marinate for several hours or overnight at room temperature. There's no need to refrigerate.

● Preheat the oven to 450°. Fit half the dough into a 10-inch tart pan with a removable bottom.

● Using a slotted spoon, transfer the lemon slices to the crust, leaving as much of the syrup in the bowl as possible. Arrange the lemon slices in an even layer. Sprinkle the remaining ¹/₃ cup sugar evenly over the slices.

● Add 5 eggs to the lemon syrup in the bowl and beat well, until the eggs are light yellow in color. Pour the egg mixture evenly over the lemons.

● Beat the remaining egg well with 1 tablespoon water. Brush the edge of the bottom crust with some of the egg mixture.

● Cut 3 vents in the top crust and fit it over the tart. Crimp the edges together to seal, and brush the edges and top lightly with the remaining egg mixture.

● Place the tart on a baking sheet and bake for 15 minutes. Lower the oven temperature to 350° and bake for 35 to 40 minutes longer or until a knife inserted through one of the vents comes out clean. Cool completely and lift the tart from the pan, leaving the bottom in place.

MAKES 8 TO 10 SERVINGS.

BO AND BILLIE: A LOVELY SCHOOL LUNCH

When Billie Reed came to town, she had problems with money, drugs, and prostitution. Carrie, who was in love with Billie's brother Austin, took her in. Carrie's uncle Bo got Billie a job at Casey's Roadhouse—the first of many kindnesses he would do for her. As a result, Billie fell in love with Bo, but it wasn't until Bo's longtime lover, Dr. Carly Manning, left town that Billie began to hope that it might someday be reciprocated. The two were brought closer together while in Los Angeles tracking down a sniper, who in reality was Billie's father, Curtis. Back in Salem, Billie was accused of Curtis's murder and Bo came to her rescue by putting up the *Fancy Face* as collateral for her bail bond. Although Billie was proven innocent, the degradation and abuse she had suffered at her father's hands as a child came to light, making Billie feel worthless and lose her hope of keeping Bo. But to Billie's complete amazement, Bo stood by her side. Even more surprisingly, Bo gallantly romanced her as if he were Billie's first love. Bo did everything in his power to build Billie's self-esteem, including sending her back to high school to earn a diploma. On her first day of school—an extremely nerve-racking day for Billie—Bo chivalrously packed her a very grown-up, incredibly fabulous school lunch.

MENU

❧

ARTICHOKE ORZO SALAD WITH GRILLED CHICKEN
OR SHRIMP

BABY CARROTS AND CELERY STICKS
WITH YOGURT DILL DRESSING

"I LOVE YOU" COOKIES

Artichoke orzo salad with grilled chicken or shrimp

This salad works well for just about any add-in. Substitute roasted chicken or boiled shrimp if that's what you've got. Or use roasted vegetables.

$1/2$	pound orzo (rice-shaped pasta)
1	tablespoon plus $1/4$ teaspoon salt or to taste
1	tablespoon lemon juice
1	(9-ounce) package frozen or 1 (9$1/2$-ounce) can artichoke hearts
1	Roma tomato, seeded and chopped
2	tablespoons chopped fresh basil, fresh parsley, or green onions (green part only)
1	cup bite-size pieces of grilled or roasted chicken, boiled or grilled shrimp, or roasted vegetables
2	tablespoons olive oil
1	tablespoon lemon juice
$1/4$	teaspoon black pepper or to taste

 Bring a large potful of water to a boil. Add 1 tablespoon salt and the pasta. Cook just until the pasta is tender, about 8 to 10 minutes. Drain well and place in a large bowl.

 Thaw according to package directions or drain and rinse canned artichoke hearts. Chop coarsely and add to the pasta, along with the tomato. Add the basil, parsley, or green onions as desired, and the chicken, shrimp, or roasted vegetables (or any combination).

● Toss to distribute the ingredients evenly. Stir together the olive oil, lemon juice, ¼ teaspoon salt, and pepper to taste. Pour over the pasta and toss to coat well. Keep cool or in an insulated lunch bag until serving time.

MAKES 4 SERVINGS.

Yogurt dill dressing for fresh veggies

1   *(8-ounce) carton plain non-fat or low-fat yogurt*
1   *tablespoon mayonnaise (regular, low-fat, or reduced-calorie)*
½   *teaspoon salt or to taste*
¼   *teaspoon black pepper or to taste*
2   *tablespoons chopped fresh dill (parsley or green onions)*

● In a small bowl, combine the yogurt, mayonnaise, salt, pepper, and chopped herb (or a combination). Store in the refrigerator for up to 3 days. Serve with fresh vegetables for dipping or as a salad dressing.

MAKES ABOUT 1 CUP.

"I love you" cookies

Sugar cookies (see recipe on page 104)
1   *batch sugar cookie frosting (see recipe on page 105)*

● Make your own sugar cookies or use refrigerated sugar-cookie dough and ready-made decorator frosting.

● Decorate the cookies with your message of choice: "Good luck." "Love, Bo." "XOXO."

JACK AND JENNIFER'S ROMANTIC PICNIC

Jack Deveraux and Jennifer Horton Deveraux Blake bring to mind Spencer Tracy and Katharine Hepburn in the classic film *Woman of the Year*. Jack was the gruff, experienced editor of *The Salem Spectator*; Jennifer was the classy younger woman who had much to learn about the real world. The chemistry between them was extraordinary, and as much as Jack tried to deny it, the two proved to be a match made in heaven. But, like most couples, they had problems, too. Jack's biological father and his adoptive father both were violent men, and Jennifer's mother and grandmother were mentally unstable. And it wasn't long after the star-struck pair first made love (while stranded on an island after the ship they were on was sunk by Ernesto Toscano) that Jennifer was raped by Lawrence Alamain. As a result, she turned down Jack's marriage proposal, a proposal she eventually accepted. Jack almost missed his wedding and was swindled out of his fortune, but the stalwart Jennifer stood by his side. On the last night in their penthouse apartment, Jack and Jennifer had a romantic indoor picnic. It was on that special evening that Jennifer told Jack she was pregnant with Abigail. Now what could be more loving than that?

M E N U

CHICKEN ROSEMARY

SOUR CREAM POTATO SALAD

SUGAR SNAP PEAS AND YOGURT DILL DRESSING
(SEE RECIPE ON PAGE 31)

LUSCIOUS CHOCOLATE CAKE

Chicken rosemary

This dish may be served hot or cold.

4   skinless, boneless chicken breasts, fresh or thawed
1/4   cup olive oil
1   teaspoon garlic seasoning blend or to taste
2   teaspoons dried rosemary or 2 tablespoons fresh
1   teaspoon coarsely ground black pepper or to taste

- Rinse and dry the chicken breasts. If uneven thickness, place the breasts between pieces of waxed paper and gently pound with the bottom of a glass or a rolling pin to the same thickness. Place the breasts in a resealable plastic food bag.

- Measure the olive oil in an 8-ounce measuring cup. Add the garlic seasoning blend, rosemary, and black pepper. Stir to combine. Pour over the chicken and seal the bag, squeezing out air. Turn the bag several times to coat the chicken breasts evenly with the marinade. Refrigerate at least 1 hour or overnight. When ready to cook, remove from the marinade and drain any excess.

- Chicken may be grilled over medium-hot coals, broiled in the oven, or cooked in a skillet on top of the stove. To check for doneness, pierce the breasts with the tip of a sharp knife. If the juices run clear, the breasts are done. Boneless, skinless breasts cook fast. Do not overcook to prevent drying.

- *To grill:* Prepare the coals and allow to burn down until well-covered with gray ash. Place the chicken breasts on the grill and cook until juices run clear, turning once, about 5 to 7 minutes.

- *To broil:* Preheat the oven broiler. Place the chicken breasts on a broiler pan and cook

until juices run clear, turning once, about 5 to 7 minutes.

- *To sauté:* Heat a large skillet over medium-high heat. Place the chicken breasts in the hot skillet and cook until juices run clear, turning once, about 5 to 7 minutes. Serve warm or slightly chilled.

- For easier serving at a picnic, cut the chicken breasts into thin slices.

MAKES 4 SERVINGS.

JENNIFER HORTON DEVERAUX BLAKE

Born in a farmhouse during a snowstorm, Jennifer is the daughter of Drs. Bill and Laura Horton and the younger sister of Mike Horton, also a doctor. When Laura was institutionalized, Bill placed Jennifer in the care of grandparents Tom and Alice Horton. After a brief period as a rebellious teen, Jennifer got her act together, began studying journalism in college, and was hired as a newspaper intern by Diana Colville. Jennifer found her true calling—and her first husband, Jack Deveraux—at The Salem Spectator. Although there previously had been men in her life, including Frankie Brady and Emilio Ramirez, none stirred her passion like Jack. Theirs was a difficult courtship and marriage. Jennifer tried to stand by her man, but Jack made that impossible. So when suave, smooth-talking Peter Blake entered the picture and promised to take care of her and daughter Abby, Jennifer fell prey to his charms. Despite her mother's warnings, Jennifer married Peter on the rebound. But those who marry in haste repent in leisure, as Jennifer found out. After believing for some time that Peter had died, she began to have doubts. Jennifer's most terrifying thought is that Peter is still alive and will become obsessed with her, just as Stefano DiMera is obsessed with Marlena Evans. If that's the case, Jack may stay in prison forever, and the Deveraux family will never be reunited.

Sour cream potato salad

1   pound (2 to 3) russet potatoes
2 ½ teaspoons salt, divided
¼   cup mayonnaise
⅓   cup sour cream
1   tablespoon capers, well-drained
1   tablespoon minced chives or green onion tops
1   teaspoon black pepper or to taste
2   hard-boiled eggs, divided (optional)
¼   cup finely chopped parsley

- Place the potatoes in a large saucepan with enough cold water to cover. Add 2 teaspoons salt and bring water to a boil over high heat. Cook until the potatoes are easily pierced with a fork all the way to the middle, about 20 to 30 minutes, depending on the size of the potatoes.

- Drain the potatoes and cool enough to handle easily.

- Remove peels and cut the potatoes into bite-size cubes, about 1-inch square. Place in a large bowl.

JACK DEVERAUX

As the old saying goes, The love of a good woman can turn a man around. And Jack Deveraux, the adopted son of Anjelica and Harper Deveraux, is a case in point. The Jack who

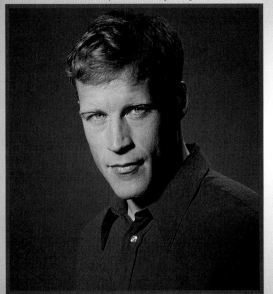

came to Salem in 1987 suffering from Hodgkin's disease just isn't the same person we've since come to know and love. It wasn't until Jack met Jennifer Rose Horton that he began to change into the man he is today— one his birth mother, Jo Johnson, would be proud of. The old Jack's crimes included raping his wife Kayla, breaking Harper out of jail to get his hands on Harper's Swiss bank account, and blackmailing his way into owning half of The Salem Spectator. The day that Jennifer joined the newspaper's staff as a college intern was a turning point in Jack's life. He found love, married, had a beautiful daughter, and then left town, overcome by guilt from believing he was the cause of Abby's aplastic anemia. Jack returned a reformed man—one who had finally learned the meaning of true love—and has struggled to put the pieces of his life back together. He stands a good chance of doing so, if Stefano DiMera and Peter Blake will just leave him alone.

- Stir together the mayonnaise, sour cream, capers, chives, and black pepper. If using eggs, separate the yolk and white of one egg and finely chop each. Gently blend into dressing.

- Fold the dressing into the potatoes and toss gently to coat the ingredients evenly. Add ½ teaspoon salt or to taste.

- Cut the remaining hard-boiled egg into thin rounds or wedges and use to decorate the top edges of the potato salad. Sprinkle with chopped parsley and chill for at least 1 hour.

MAKES 4 SERVINGS.

Luscious chocolate cake

This is a flourless chocolate cake—dense, luxurious, intense, and oh, so chocolaty.

10   *ounces bittersweet chocolate*
1½ *sticks butter*
2   *teaspoons vanilla extract*
5   *eggs*
1   *cup sugar*
Confectioners' sugar for garnish
Fresh raspberries for garnish

- Preheat the oven to 350˚. Lightly rub butter onto the bottom and sides of a 9-inch diameter springform pan. Line the pan bottom with a piece of parchment paper, waxed paper, or foil. Trim edges to fit the bottom.

- Chop the chocolate and cut the butter into pieces. Place the chocolate and butter in a small saucepan over medium-low heat. Stir and heat until the mixture is smooth. Remove from heat and allow to cool slightly. Stir in the vanilla.

- In a large bowl, combine the eggs and sugar. Using electric beaters, beat on medium-high until the mixture lightens in color and texture and the volume triples, about 5 to 6 minutes. Add the chocolate to the egg mixture, using a rubber spatula to blend gently. Pour the batter into the prepared pan.

- Bake until the top forms a crust and cracks, about 45 minutes. A tester inserted into the center should come out with some moist batter still attached. Remove the cake and place on a rack to cool. Run a knife around the edges to loosen the sides. Do not worry if the cake falls in the middle. It is supposed to. Press down around the edges to even the top. Cool completely.

- Release the pan sides and remove. Invert the cake on a serving platter. Lift off the pan bottom and peel off the parchment, foil, or waxed paper.

- Refrigerate until serving time. When ready to serve, sift confectioners' sugar over the top and decorate with fresh raspberries.

MAKES 10 SERVINGS.

Vivian and Ivan's Elegant Meal

Vivian Alamain and Ivan Marais are not the usual romantic soap-opera couple, but they do lend a great deal of comic relief to life in Salem. Vivian lusts after Victor Kiriakis, and Ivan pines for his "Madame." Vivian, of course, is aware of Ivan's amorous bent and constantly uses it to get him to pamper and please her. There have been a few times when Ivan thought he was finally going to make love to the object of his desire, only to be thwarted. In Paris, Ivan surprised his true love with a sentimental dinner for two— candlelight, champagne, caviar—but was replaced at the last moment by Stefano DiMera, who was pretending to be Rudolfo, a lover from Vivian's past. Later, back in Salem, Ivan tricked Vivian into thinking he needed to have sex to cure him after he was accidentally injected with an anti-lactation shot that Dr. Wu had intended for Susan Banks. Vivian discovered the ruse at the last moment and taught Ivan a lesson by having Olga show up in her place. Nevertheless, Ivan had set the scene for seduction. You can, too, if you take your cue from the menu that follows.

M E N U

HEARTS OF PALM WITH CHAMPAGNE VINAIGRETTE

LAMB CHOPS CRUSTED WITH
VIVIAN'S FAVORITE HERB BLEND

EROS' ORZO WITH SUN-DRIED TOMATOES
AND IVAN'S PESTO

CREAMED SPINACH

BITTERSWEET COEUR À LA CRÈME WITH AMARETTO SAUCE

TRUFFLES

Hearts of palm salad

1	(14-ounce) can hearts of palm, chilled
1	large avocado
1	tablespoon lemon juice or as needed
1	Roma tomato
$^{1}/_{2}$	teaspoon salt or to taste
1	teaspoon freshly cracked pepper or to taste

Champagne Vinaigrette (recipe follows)

- Drain the hearts of palm and cut into 1-inch pieces. Peel and seed the avocado. Cut into $^{1}/_{2}$-inch cubes; toss the avocado with lemon juice to prevent it from turning brown. Cut off the ends of the tomato and gently but firmly squeeze out as many seeds as possible. Chop the tomato into confetti-size pieces.

- Toss together the hearts of palm, avocado, and tomato; add salt and pepper to taste. Pour just enough Champagne Vinaigrette over the salad to coat the ingredients and toss well.

MAKES 4 SERVINGS.

Champagne vinaigrette

$^{1}/_{2}$	cup mild-flavored extra-virgin olive oil
3	tablespoons champagne vinegar
1	tablespoon finely chopped shallots
$^{1}/_{4}$	teaspoon salt or to taste
$^{1}/_{4}$	teaspoon freshly cracked black pepper or to taste

- Combine the oil, vinegar, shallots, salt, and pepper in a jar with a tight-fitting lid or in a small bowl. Shake until well-blended or mix with a wire whisk. Pour over salad.

MAKES ABOUT ³/₄ CUP.

Lamb chops crusted with Vivian's favorite herb blend

6   (1¹/₂-inch-thick) lamb chops
¹/₄   cup Vivian's Favorite Herb Blend (recipe follows)
¹/₂   cup dry breadcrumbs
1   teaspoon salt or to taste, divided
1   teaspoon freshly cracked pepper or to taste, divided
¹/₄   cup extra-virgin olive oil

- Rinse and dry the lamb chops. Combine the herb blend, breadcrumbs, ¹/₂ teaspoon salt, and ¹/₂ teaspoon pepper in a pie plate. Stir to blend.

- Brush the lamb chops with olive oil on all sides. Holding a lamb chop by the bone, dip the thick edge (the opposite side parallel to the bone) into the herb mixture and pat the herb mixture in to adhere. Season the uncoated sides of the lamb chop with salt and pepper to taste.

- Heat a heavy-bottomed skillet over medium-high heat. When the pan is almost smoking, add a thin coating of olive oil. Place 3 lamb chops in the skillet and cook on one side until well-browned. Turn and cook on the other side until the desired degree of doneness is reached, preferably medium rare (red, warm center). Keep warm. Repeat with the remaining lamb chops. Serve warm or at room temperature.

MAKES 2 SERVINGS.

Vivian's favorite herb blend

¹/₄   cup dried leaf parsley
¹/₄   cup dried leaf thyme
¹/₄   cup dried marjoram
4   medium bay leaves, crushed
3   tablespoons dried leaf oregano
1   tablespoon dried rosemary
1   teaspoon dried lemon rind
1   teaspoon dried tarragon
¹/₈   teaspoon cayenne pepper

- Combine all ingredients in a mixing bowl and stir well to combine. Store in an airtight container on a dark shelf, away from heat and moisture.

- Herb blend may be added to soups, stews, and vegetables; blended into soft cheeses; and stirred into liquid marinades for fish, poultry, beef, pork, or lamb. Use about 1 tablespoon herbs per cup of liquid.

MAKES ABOUT 1 CUP.

Cooking for Romance

Eros' orzo with sun–dried tomatoes and Ivan's pesto

1   cup orzo (rice-shaped pasta)
1¹/₂ teaspoons salt or to taste, divided
2 to 3 sun-dried tomatoes (packed in oil)
1   (8-ounce) package frozen green peas
3   tablespoons Ivan's Pesto (recipe follows) or to taste

● Bring a medium-size potful of water to a boil over high heat. Stir in the orzo and 1 teaspoon salt. Cook the pasta according to package directions or until tender but still firm to the bite, about 10 minutes. Meanwhile, place the frozen peas in a colander. When the pasta is done, pour the cooking water over the peas to drain the pasta and thaw the peas.

● Drain the oil from the sun-dried tomatoes and cut into thin strips or small pieces. Toss with the pasta and peas. Lightly coat with Ivan's Pesto. Serve warm or at room temperature.

MAKES 3 TO 4 SERVINGS.

Cooking for Romance

Ivan's pesto

1¹/₃ *cups fresh parsley leaves*
1   *clove garlic or 2 teaspoons finely chopped garlic*
¹/₃   *cup pine nuts (pignoli)*
²/₃   *cup finely shredded fresh Parmesan cheese*
²/₃   *cup extra-virgin olive oil*

● In the work bowl of a food processor or a blender container, combine the parsley, garlic, and pine nuts. Process, using pulse or on-off switch, until the ingredients are finely chopped.

● Add the cheese and process until thick and well blended. With the motor running, slowly add the olive oil and process until it becomes the consistency of creamed butter.

● Use the pesto to lightly coat the orzo or other pasta. Store the remainder in the refrigerator for up to 2 weeks or freeze.

MAKES ABOUT 1¹/₂ CUPS.

VIVIAN ALAMAIN AND IVAN MARAIS

A passionate woman, Vivian loves the royal life to which she was born and she's infatuated with Victor Kiriakis. Her problem is that she's not above bending the law to achieve her goals. Her deeds are legendary: She stole Nicky from Carly Manning at birth and later buried Carly alive after ruining Carly's reputation as a doctor by murdering her patients. She stole Kate Roberts's embryo and had it implanted into her own uterus. She blackmailed Kristen Blake, and she tricked Victor into marrying her so he couldn't marry Kate. It's no wonder that the only person in Salem who wants to have anything to do with

Vivian is her loyal manservant and partner in crime, Ivan Marais. Ivan's love for his "Madame" has made him an accomplished expert on grave digging, infertility, Chinese herbs, and cross-dressing. Vivian leads and Ivan follows, constantly putting his life and limbs at risk.

Creamed spinach

To make a double batch, follow the directions in parentheses.

1	(2) (10-ounce) package(s) frozen chopped spinach
1	(2) tablespoon(s) butter
1/4	(1/2) cup chopped onion
1/3	(2/3) cup sour cream
1/4	(1/2) teaspoon salt or to taste
1/8	(1/4) teaspoon grated nutmeg

- Cook the spinach according to the package directions and drain well. Place in a colander and press with the back of a spoon to remove excess liquid.

- In a medium saucepan over medium heat, combine the butter and onion and cook until the onion is soft, 3 to 5 minutes.

- Stir in the spinach, sour cream, salt, and nutmeg. Heat throughout but do not allow to boil or the sour cream will curdle.

MAKES 2 (4) SERVINGS.

Bittersweet coeur à la crème

2	ounces bittersweet chocolate
2	(3-ounce) packages cream cheese, softened to room temperature
1/4	cup confectioners' sugar
1	teaspoon vanilla extract

Pinch of salt

1/2	cup whipping cream
1	cup fresh strawberries or raspberries for garnish

Amaretto Sauce (recipe follows)
Ginger snaps or crackers (from the supermarket or gourmet store)

- Line a 2-cup heart-shaped mold or a coeur à la crème dish with wet cheesecloth. If a heart-shaped mold is not available, any round mold or bowl will do.

- Place the chocolate in a small bowl and microwave on High for 30 seconds; stir. If more cooking time is needed to melt the chocolate, microwave on High for 10 seconds at a time, stirring after each interval, until chocolate is melted. Allow to cool.

- Place the cream cheese in a medium mixing bowl and beat with an electric mixer until fluffy. Add the melted chocolate, using a rubber spatula to scrape all the chocolate into the bowl. Stir in the sugar, vanilla, and salt. Beat well to combine.

- Place the cream in a small bowl and beat with an electric mixer until soft peaks form. Using a rubber spatula, beat a small amount of the cream cheese into the whipped cream, then fold the whipped cream mixture into the cream cheese. Pour into the cheesecloth-lined mold.

Refrigerate overnight. Using the edges of the cheesecloth, lift out the molded chocolate-cheese mixture. Invert onto a serving tray and peel off the cheesecloth. Surround with strawberries or raspberries. Drizzle Amaretto Sauce over the bittersweet chocolate coeur à la crème. Serve as a chocolate spread with ginger snaps, cookies, or crackers.

MAKES 4 SERVINGS.

Amaretto sauce

$^1/_2$ cup sugar
1   tablespoon cornstarch
Pinch of salt
1   cup boiling water
1   tablespoon butter
1   tablespoon amaretto (almond) liqueur
$^1/_4$ teaspoon vanilla extract

In a small saucepan over medium heat, combine the sugar, cornstarch, salt, and boiling water. Stirring constantly, cook until the mixture becomes clear. Remove from heat and stir in the butter, amaretto, and vanilla. Serve at room temperature. Store in the refrigerator.

MAKES 1 CUP.

Truffles

1¹/₂ to 1³/₄ pounds semisweet chocolate, divided
1¹/₂ cups heavy cream
1¹/₂ tablespoons vanilla, cognac, brandy, bourbon,
orange liqueur such as Grand Marnier, or
almond liqueur such as amaretto

- Chop ¹/₂ pound of the chocolate into small pieces. Combine the chopped chocolate with the cream in the top of a double boiler over simmering water. Stir occasionally, until melted and smooth. Remove from heat and allow to cool slightly.

- Stir in the vanilla or other flavoring, as desired. Cover and refrigerate until very thick, at least 5 hours or overnight.

- Shape the chocolate mixture into small balls, using a generous tablespoon of chocolate. The balls should be somewhat rough and irregular, not perfectly round.

- Place the chocolate balls on a pastry sheet lined with aluminum foil or waxed paper. Freeze for several hours or overnight.

- To coat the balls with melted chocolate, melt the remaining chocolate (1 to 1¹/₄ pounds) in the top of a double boiler over simmering— not boiling—water. If using a candy thermometer, do not allow the temperature of the chocolate to exceed 90°.

- Remove from heat and let the chocolate cool to lukewarm.

- Meanwhile, line 2 cookie sheets with waxed paper or aluminum foil. When the chocolate is cool enough, spear a truffle on a fork and dip it into the lukewarm chocolate, turning to coat evenly. Allow excess chocolate to drip back into the pan.

- Carefully scrape the bottom of the truffle against the pan to prevent a puddle of chocolate from forming around the bottom. Using the side of a knife, slide the truffle onto a prepared cookie sheet. Repeat the process with the remaining truffles, placing them in the refrigerator as soon as possible.

- Chill until firm, about 1 hour. Cover lightly with aluminum foil or waxed paper. Store in the refrigerator for up to 6 weeks.

MAKES ABOUT 36 TRUFFLES.

2 HOT SPOTS OF SALEM

Being all dressed up with nowhere to go is not a problem for the residents of Salem. The city offers a host of attractive options for dining, entertainment, and celebrations. For an upscale night on the town, the place to see and be seen is the Penthouse Grill, where patrons can enjoy a lush gourmet meal and an unparalleled view of the city and its glittering lights. Want a private tête-à-tête with your cher amour? Chez Vous provides exquisite French cuisine and an intimate atmosphere. Feel like grabbing a beer and dancing the two-step? The doors of the Cheatin' Heart are always open. If you're doing some after-work shopping at Salem Place, there's no place more convenient than Johnny Angel's for a sumptuous burger and fries. Craving a warm, family atmosphere? Shawn and Caroline Brady will provide that and some great clam chowder at the Brady Pub. And before making the rounds of their favorite establishments, many of Salem's leading couples and singles are sure to head for the Titan Gym to buff up their bodies and enjoy a healthy protein shake at the Juice Bar.

PENTHOUSE GRILL

Wings crashed and burned, the Salem Club was in today and gone even quicker, and the Snake Pit's service was arrested along with drug lord JL King. Now, the Penthouse Grill sits high atop the Titan Industries Building, and those in the know have pronounced it *the* place to dine for Salem's movers and shakers. The elegant establishment is exquisitely decorated in subtle, warm, and flattering colors; its tables are set with beautiful china, silver, and crystal; and the lush floral arrangements are always fresh. The food is divine and the service is exceptional. Windows surrounding the restaurant offer a breathtaking, panoramic view of the city, and there's also a terrace where patrons can adjourn for a breath of fresh air or to share a private moment with that special someone. The Penthouse Grill is where John Black and Marlena Evans held their engagement party, Hope Brady and Franco Kelly charmed there way into a major advertising campaign, and Vivian Alamain danced her way into the hospital. It's also Abe and Lexie Carver's favorite place when they're out for a night on the town.

MENU

CRAB CAKES OVER SEASONAL GREENS
WITH MUSTARD TARTAR SAUCE

KC STRIP WITH PEPPERCORN PAN SAUCE

SMASHED GARLIC POTATOES

ROASTED SEASONAL VEGETABLES

BANANAS FLAMBÉ WITH VANILLA ICE CREAM

Crab cakes over seasonal greens with mustard tartar sauce

Nothing starts a meal better than crab cakes. For some Penthouse Grill regulars, this signature dish is the meal.

1   *pound fresh lump crabmeat (not artificial crab)*
2   *tablespoons mayonnaise*
2   *tablespoons Dijon mustard*
2   *eggs*
1/3 *cup fresh breadcrumbs*
1   *tablespoon finely chopped green onions (white and green parts)*
1/8 *teaspoon cayenne pepper or to taste*
1/2 *teaspoon salt or to taste*
1/4 *teaspoon black pepper or to taste*
1   *cup dry breadcrumbs*
About *1/2 cup vegetable oil*
Mustard Tartar Sauce (recipe follows)
2 to 3 cups assorted field greens or mesclun salad blend
2 to 3 tablespoons balsamic vinegar

 Carefully pick over the crab, removing any shell or cartilage. Combine the mayonnaise, 2 tablespoons mustard, and the eggs in a medium bowl. Whisk together to mix well. Add the crab, fresh breadcrumbs, onion, cayenne, salt, and black pepper. Mix well to distribute ingredients evenly.

44

- Divide the mixture into 12 oval cakes about ¹/₂-inch thick.

- Dip the crab cakes into the dry breadcrumbs, gently pressing crumbs into all sides of the crab cakes. Set aside on waxed paper.

- Heat ¹/₄ inch vegetable oil in a large skillet over medium heat until very hot, almost smoking. Carefully slide the crab cakes into the hot oil. Do not allow sides to touch. Cook in several batches, adding more oil as needed.

- Cook the crab cakes for 2 to 4 minutes on each side or until golden brown. Serve hot with a dollop of Mustard Tartar Sauce and greens drizzled with balsamic vinegar.

**MAKES 4 SERVINGS
(3 CRAB CAKES PER SERVING).**

Mustard tartar sauce

¹/₂   cup bottled tartar sauce
2   tablespoons Dijon mustard

- In a small bowl, combine the tartar sauce and the mustard. Stir until well-mixed.

KC strip with peppercorn pan sauce

4   (6-ounce) top loin strips (preferably Certified
        Angus Beef)
2   teaspoons steak seasoning blend (your favorite)
        or to taste
1   teaspoon finely chopped garlic (optional)
$1/2$ cup beef broth
$1/2$ cup dry red wine
1   tablespoon peppercorns (green, pink, or a
        multi-color blend)
$1/2$ teaspoon salt or to taste
$1/2$ teaspoon black pepper or to taste
1 to 2 tablespoons butter (optional)

● Heat a heavy-bottom skillet (preferably cast iron) over high heat until very hot, almost smoking. Place 1 or 2 steaks, depending on size, in the skillet and cook until dark brown around the edges.

● Turn and cook the other side until dark brown. Test for doneness by firmly, but gently and quickly, touching the steak in the thickest part with your forefinger. If the steak has the same "give" as the thickest part of your palm right below the thumb, it is medium rare (warm center). Remove to a platter and keep warm.

● Repeat with the remaining steaks. If steaks are preferred cooked longer, lower heat to medium and return the steaks to the pan. Cook to the

ABE AND LEXIE CARVER

Abe is the Commander of the Salem Police Department. Lexie is a medical student who used to be a cop, until she was caught helping Abe's brother Jonah (about whom she was having fantasies) in his efforts to clean up Salem in the guise of the "Pacifier." When Abe was forced to suspend her for her illegal activities, Lexie got over her obsession and got on with her life. Then, in the mysterious town of Aremid, Lexie uncovered secrets about herself—that her birth mother was Celeste Perrault and her father was none other than the evil Stefano DiMera. Now she worries about the role DNA plays in determining character and whether she should give birth to a child who could be genetically sinful.

desired degree of doneness. Steaks cooked more than medium (very little pink in the center) are not recommended.

- Season the steaks on both sides with the steak seasoning blend and keep warm.

- Pour off as much fat from the pan as possible. Return the pan to medium heat. Add the garlic and stir. Cook for 1 to 2 minutes or just until the garlic releases its aroma and begins to brown around the edges.

- Pour in the beef broth and wine. Bring the liquid to a boil, scraping up the brown bits stuck to the bottom of the pan using a wooden spoon. Boil until the liquid is reduced by half, about 4 minutes.

- For a more professional sauce, pour the sauce through a strainer and return to the pan. Reduce heat to simmer.

- Add the peppercorns, salt, and pepper to taste. If desired, add the butter, stirring constantly with a wire whisk. Do not allow to boil again. Remove from heat. Pour over the steaks to serve.

MAKES 4 SERVINGS.

Smashed garlic potatoes

2   pounds (approximately 4) russet potatoes
4   cloves fresh garlic, peeled
Water
1   tablespoon salt or to taste
2   tablespoons unsalted butter
About $\frac{1}{2}$ cup warm milk
$\frac{1}{2}$ teaspoon pepper or to taste

● Peel the potatoes and cut into quarters or eighths, depending on size. Place the potatoes and garlic in a large saucepan with enough water to cover. Over high heat, bring the water to a boil. Add up to 1 tablespoon salt.

● When the liquid boils, reduce heat to low; cover and cook until the potatoes are easily pierced with a fork, about 20 minutes.

● Drain the potatoes, reserving about $\frac{1}{2}$ cup of the cooking liquid. Return the potatoes to the saucepan over low heat. Shaking the pan, cook the potatoes for 2 to 3 minutes to allow liquid to evaporate. Remove from heat and place on a thick towel that has been folded several times.

● Using a potato masher, begin breaking up the potatoes. Add the butter and continue mashing. When most of the big lumps have disappeared, begin adding the warm milk. Continue mashing until the mixture is smooth.

● For an even smoother mixture, use electric beaters. If more liquid is needed for the desired consistency, gradually add enough cooking liquid to thin the potatoes. Add the pepper and adjust seasoning with salt as needed.

MAKES 4 TO 6 SERVINGS.

Roasted seasonal vegetables

Depending on the season, this side dish may contain potatoes, carrots, fresh beets, turnips, sugar snap peas, yellow squash, baby tomatoes, or zucchini, or a combination of several. Follow the roasting times indicated.

4 to 6 cups vegetables, such as unpeeled new potatoes or
    russet potatoes (cut into quarters); peeled sweet
    potatoes (cut into quarters or eighths); baby carrots,
    baby beets, small turnips, sugar snap peas, yellow
    squash, or zucchini (cut into 2-inch pieces); cherry
    or cocktail tomatoes (see roasting times below)
$1/2$ cup olive oil or as needed
$1^1/2$ teaspoons salt or to taste
1   teaspoon pepper or to taste
1   tablespoon lemon juice or to taste

- Preheat the oven to 375°. Rinse, dry, and cut the vegetables for roasting. Vegetables should be approximately the same size. Spray a 9x13-inch baking dish with cooking spray.

- Toss the vegetables with olive oil to coat evenly (or spray with olive oil spray). Roast the vegetables in stages, beginning with those requiring the longest time in the oven. Add others as the remaining cooking time decreases.

  Potatoes (all varieties), turnips—30 minutes

  Baby carrots, baby beets—20 minutes

  Yellow squash, zucchini—15 minutes

  Sugar snap peas, cherry or cocktail tomatoes—10 minutes

- Additional cooking time (as much as 10 to 15 minutes) may be required if the oven has been opened frequently to add additional vegetables. Cook the vegetables to the desired degree of doneness. Add more olive oil if the vegetables appear dry.

- Season to taste with salt and pepper. Sprinkle lightly with lemon juice before serving.

MAKES 4 TO 6 SERVINGS.

Bananas flambé with vanilla ice cream

4   ripe, but not mushy, bananas
1   tablespoon lemon juice
1   stick unsalted butter
$1/2$ cup firmly packed brown sugar
1   teaspoon vanilla extract
$1/4$ cup rum, bourbon or brandy, heated
4   scoops Vanity Vanilla Ice Cream (see recipe on
    page 166) or store-bought
Mint leaves for garnish (optional)

- Peel the bananas and cut in half. Divide each piece lengthwise. Sprinkle with lemon juice and set aside.

- In a large skillet over medium heat, combine the butter and the brown sugar, stirring gently. When the butter and brown sugar are melted and well combined, add the bananas and cook for 2 to 3 minutes, basting the bananas with the butter mixture.

- Add the vanilla. Pour the heated spirits over the bananas. Cook for 2 to 3 minutes to evaporate the alcohol. If desired, touch a lighted match to the surface as soon as the alcohol is added. Use caution! Lighting the alcohol can cause blue flames to shoot into the air. Have a lid ready to smother the flames. Allow the flames to burn for 5 to 10 seconds before smothering.

- Remove the bananas from heat and leave covered to keep warm. To serve, spoon the bananas over scoops of Vanity Vanilla Ice Cream or store-bought. Garnish with mint leaves, if desired.

MAKES 4 SERVINGS.

CHEZ VOUS

The lights are low, the mood is intimate, the music is sentimental, and the accent is French. Chez Vous is the restaurant for lovers: John and Marlena, Jack and Jennifer, Carrie and Austin—and yes!—even Carrie and Mike. If you can't be in Paris, what could be more sublime than a night of romance at Salem's premier French bistro?

M E N U

CREAM OF MUSHROOM SOUP

SEA BASS WITH A MUSTARD CRUST AND LEMON BUTTER

POTATOES CHEZ VOUS

BABY CARROTS

WATERCRESS SALAD

APPLE (OR PLUM) CAKE

Cream of mushroom soup

This classic French soup is a favorite at Chez Vous. Regulars wouldn't dream of coming in without having a cup.

$^1/_2$ *stick unsalted butter*
$^1/_2$ *cup finely chopped onion*
$^1/_2$ *pound finely chopped fresh mushrooms**
1   *tablespoon all-purpose flour*
2   *cups chicken broth*
1   *teaspoon dried thyme*
$^3/_4$ *cup cream or milk*
1   *teaspoon salt or to taste*
$^1/_2$ *teaspoon pepper or to taste*
Fresh thyme leaves for garnish (optional)

● In a large saucepan over low heat, melt the butter. Add the onion and mushrooms. Cook for 15 minutes, stirring occasionally. Sprinkle with the flour and cook for 2 to 3 minutes longer, stirring occasionally.

● Add the chicken broth gradually, stirring constantly. Raise heat to medium and allow the liquid to come to a boil. Reduce heat; add the thyme and simmer for 20 minutes. Stir in the cream. Add salt and pepper to taste. Heat throughout, but do not boil.

MAKES 6 SERVINGS.

*Note: Use white mushrooms or a combination of any mushrooms you choose. Wild mushrooms, such as morels, give a rich, earthy flavor to the soup. If using dried wild mushrooms, soak them in just enough hot water to cover for 30 minutes to make chopping easier. Add the soaking liquid to the soup.

Sea bass with mustard crust and lemon butter

4   *(6-ounce) sea bass fillets (or other whitefish fillets)*
$^1/_2$ *teaspoon salt or to taste*
$^1/_4$ *teaspoon pepper or to taste*
$^1/_2$ *cup mayonnaise or creamy salad dressing*
1   *teaspoon Dijon mustard*
1   *cup dry breadcrumbs*
1   *tablespoon grated Parmesan cheese*
2   *teaspoons lemon juice*
Lemon Butter (recipe follows)

- Preheat the oven to 400°. Spray a shallow baking dish with vegetable cooking spray.

- Rinse and dry the fish fillets. Season each fillet with salt and pepper to taste.

- Combine the mayonnaise and mustard in a small bowl, mixing well. Spread a thick layer of mustard-mayonnaise on top of each fillet.

- Combine the breadcrumbs and Parmesan cheese. Gently press a generous layer of crumbs on top of each fillet. Place the fillets in the baking dish. Sprinkle each with 1/2 teaspoon of lemon juice.

- Bake for 10 to 12 minutes or until the fish is snowy white throughout and flakes easily with a fork. Do not overcook. Cook approximately 10 minutes per inch of thickness at the thickest part. If desired, serve with a drizzle of Lemon Butter.

MAKES 4 SERVINGS.

Lemon butter

1   stick butter, melted
2 to 3 teaspoons lemon juice or to taste
2 to 3 drops red pepper sauce or to taste

- In a small saucepan, melt the butter over low heat, stirring frequently with a wire whisk. Just as the butter melts completely, stir in the lemon juice and red pepper sauce, whisking vigorously. Remove from heat and serve warm.

MAKES 1/2 CUP.

Potatoes Chez Vous

1   (28-ounce) package shredded potatoes (in the refrigerator case)*
1   tablespoon all-purpose flour
2   tablespoons butter
3/4 to 1 cup heavy cream
1   teaspoon salt or to taste
1   teaspoon pepper or to taste
1/2   teaspoon nutmeg or to taste

- Preheat the oven to 350°. Lightly spray a shallow 1 1/2-quart rectangular baking dish with vegetable cooking spray or lightly coat with butter.

- Spread the potatoes evenly in the bottom of the baking dish. Sprinkle the potatoes with the flour. Melt the butter and drizzle over the potatoes. Drizzle the cream over the potatoes. Use enough cream to coat the potatoes but not enough so the potatoes are swimming.

- Season to taste with salt, pepper, and nutmeg. Bake for 30 to 40 minutes or until lightly browned on top.

MAKES 4 TO 6 SERVINGS.

Note: To use fresh potatoes, peel and shred 3 cups potatoes. Have ready a potful of boiling water. Water should be deep enough for the potatoes to float easily. Pour the potatoes into the water. As soon as the water returns to a boil, drain the potatoes in a colander. Toss to drain as much water as possible. Proceed as above.

Baby carrots

1   (8-ounce) package baby carrots
1   teaspoon salt or to taste
2   tablespoons butter

● Place the carrots in a medium saucepan with just enough water to cover. Add the salt and place over high heat. Bring to a boil and cook just until carrots are easily pierced with a fork, about 10 minutes. Pour off the water. Add the butter and salt to taste. Keep warm.

MAKES 4 SERVINGS.

Watercress salad

2   bunches watercress, washed, dried, and stems removed
4   radishes, grated or thinly sliced
1/3 cup light olive oil or vegetable oil
1/3 cup lemon juice
2   teaspoons white vinegar
1/4 teaspoon salt or to taste

● Arrange the watercress on a large plate or on individual salad plates. Scatter the grated radish or radish slices over the watercress.

● Just before serving, combine the oil, lemon juice, vinegar, and salt in a jar with a tight-fitting lid. Shake vigorously to combine. Drizzle the dressing over the salad and serve immediately. Refrigerate any leftover dressing.

MAKES 4 SERVINGS.

Apple (or plum) cake

Depending upon what is in season, this cake may be made with apples or plums. Just make sure the latter are firm.

1/2 pound tart apples such as Granny Smith or firm red, purple, and green plums
Juice and grated rind (yellow part only) of 1 lemon, divided
2   eggs, separated
1/2 cup sugar, divided
1/2 stick unsalted butter, melted and cooled
1/2 teaspoon vanilla extract
1/3 cup all-purpose flour
1/8 teaspoon salt
Confectioners' sugar

● Preheat the oven to 375°. Cut a piece of waxed paper or baking parchment to fit the bottom of a 1-quart soufflé or baking dish. Rub butter on both sides of the paper and fit into the bottom of the dish. Rub the sides of the dish lightly with butter or spray with vegetable cooking spray.

● Peel the apples. Cut the apples into quarters (unpeeled plums in half) and remove the cores (seeds). Slice the fruit thinly. Sprinkle with half the lemon juice; set aside.

● In a medium bowl, blend the remaining lemon juice, grated lemon rind, egg yolks, 1/4 cup sugar, the cooled butter and vanilla. Add the flour and beat with a wooden spoon or electric beaters until smooth.

● In a small, clean bowl, add the salt to the egg whites and beat with clean electric beaters until soft peaks form.

Gradually add the remaining ¼ cup sugar and beat until the whites are firm enough to form stiff peaks. Stir ¼ of the egg whites into the batter. Fold in the remaining egg whites and fruit, being careful not to deflate the egg whites.

Carefully transfer the batter into the prepared mold. Smooth the top and bake for 35 to 40 minutes or until the center is set and a tester inserted in the center comes out clean. Cool for 30 minutes.

Run the tip of a sharp knife around the sides of the mold to loosen the cake. Invert over a plate and carefully remove the baking dish. Remove the paper. Allow to cool completely. Sprinkle the top generously with confectioners' sugar. Cut into slices to serve. If desired, top with whipped cream.

MAKES 4 TO 6 SERVINGS.

MIKE HORTON

The identity of Mike Horton's father was one of the longest-kept secrets on daytime television. Born as a preemie in 1968, it wasn't until an accident in 1976 that it was revealed to Mike and his father, Mickey, that Mickey's brother Bill was really Mike's biological father. By that time, Mike was working as a mechanic (the character had been aged) and fell in love with and married Margo Anderman, who was diagnosed with leukemia. In denial about her condition, Mike ran up huge debts, which limited his precious time with Margo as he worked to repay them and got Mike involved with the wrong people. Two years after Margo's death, Mike decided to follow the family tradition and enter medical school. While working at University Hospital, Mike fell in love with a nice Jewish girl, Dr. Robin Jacobs, who bore him a son, Jeremy, out of wedlock. When Robin moved to Israel, Mike followed to be close to Jeremy. On his return to Salem, he still appeared to be involved with the wrong people, including Stefano DiMera, but that situation was soon rectified. Practicing medicine isn't the only Horton tradition Mike is following; he's also fallen in love with a Brady lady.

CHEATIN' HEART

Salem's younger crowd has spent some of its happiest and saddest times
at the Cheatin' Heart. It's where Billie Reed taught Bo Brady how to two-step, Sami Brady
drugged Austin Reed's drink, and Billie, Jennifer Horton, and Kristen Blake used to go
for a girls' night out. It's also where Jack Deveraux and Hope Brady had great talks,
Billie hustled some pool games, and Austin gave Carrie a friendship ring that was a
precursor to an engagement ring. The Cheatin' Heart may not be very highbrow, but it's
a comfortable place where memories live on.

MENU

BARBECUED CHICKEN SANDWICHES

COLESLAW

HOMEMADE POTATO CHIPS

BAR-STOOL BEEF JERKY

CHOCOLATE MERINGUE PIE

Barbecued chicken sandwiches

2   (3- to 4-pound) whole chickens*
1   tablespoon salt
1   tablespoon brown sugar
1   tablespoon sugar
2   teaspoons lemon pepper
2   teaspoons garlic seasoning blend
1   teaspoon freshly ground black pepper
1   teaspoon paprika
1 to 1 ¹/2 cups bottled barbecue sauce, your favorite
8 to 10 soft, white buns, split horizontally

- Rinse and dry the chickens. Combine the salt,
  brown sugar, sugar, lemon pepper, garlic
  seasoning blend, pepper, and paprika in a small
  bowl, mixing well. Rub the seasonings into the
  cavities of the chickens and on the outside,
  coating well on all sides. Allow the chickens to
  come to room temperature, about 1 hour.

- Meanwhile, prepare the charcoal. Position the
  coals on one side of the grill and allow to burn
  down until covered with a thick coating of gray
  ash. Place the chickens on the side of the
  grilltop away from the fire. Cover and vent
  slightly to draw heat and smoke over the
  chickens.

- Carefully turn the chickens occasionally for even
  cooking and to prevent burning. Add additional
  charcoal as needed to maintain a low, steady
  temperature. Cook for about 3 to 4 hours or
  until the juices run clear when the chickens are
  pierced at the thickest part of the thigh.

- Remove the chickens from the grill and cool
  slightly. Chop or shred the meat, including
  some of the skin, if desired, for extra flavor.

- To serve, spoon some of the shredded chicken
  onto the bottom half of a bun. Add a dollop of
  barbecue sauce and Coleslaw (recipe follows),
  if desired, and cover with the bun top.

MAKES 12 TO 15 SERVINGS.

*Shortcut: Purchase barbecued chicken from the
supermarket deli or your favorite barbecue place. Shred
or chop the chicken as directed above.*

Coleslaw

2   (16-ounce) packages shredded cabbage
$^1/_2$ cup white vinegar
$^1/_3$ cup sugar
1   teaspoon salt
1   teaspoon pepper
$1^1/_2$ cups prepared mayonnaise

- Place the cabbage in a large mixing bowl. In a small bowl, stir together the vinegar, sugar, salt, and pepper until the sugar dissolves. Blend in the mayonnaise.

- Pour the dressing over the cabbage and mix well. Refrigerate for at least an hour before serving.

MAKES 10 TO 12 GARNISH SERVINGS.

Homemade potato chips

1 to 2 large russet potatoes, unpeeled
1   quart canola oil
Seasoned salt and paprika to taste

- Rinse and scrub the potatoes. Place the potatoes in ice water.

- Begin heating the oil in a deep fryer or saucepan to 475°.

- Using a thin slicing blade on a food processor, cut the potatoes into paper-thin slices. If slicing by hand, slice the potatoes as thinly as possible.

- Place the potatoes in ice water while slicing the remainder.

- When the oil is hot, shake off as much water from the potato slices as possible and blot dry with paper towels. Drop a handful of the potato slices into the hot oil. Stand back! Grease will pop.

- When the popping stops and the potatoes begin to brown, remove them with a slotted spoon or basket and drain in a single layer on paper towels. Sprinkle generously with seasoned salt and paprika.

- Keep warm. Repeat the process until all potatoes are cooked.

MAKES 2 TO 4 SERVINGS.

Bar-stool beef jerky

2	pounds round steak, at least 1-inch thick
$^1/_2$	cup soy sauce
1	teaspoon garlic seasoning blend
2	teaspoons freshly cracked black peppercorns
$^1/_4$	teaspoon cayenne pepper or to taste (optional)

- Trim all fat from the meat and cut the steak into thin strips, about $^1/_4$-inch thick and 3 to 4 inches long. Place the strips in a resealable plastic bag.

- In a large measuring cup, combine the soy sauce, garlic seasoning blend, black pepper, and cayenne pepper, if desired. Pour over the meat strips. Squeeze out air and seal the bag. Turn the bag several times and move around the meat and sauce to make sure all strips are well-coated with marinade.

- Refrigerate overnight. Remove the bag from the refrigerator 1 hour before drying in the oven.

- Preheat the oven to 175°. Line a cookie sheet with foil. Remove the meat from the marinade and shake off any excess liquid. Discard the remaining marinade.

- Arrange the meat strips flat in a single layer on the cookie sheet. If desired, press cracked black peppercorns from the marinade into the surface of the meat. Place the cookie sheet in the oven for 1 hour. Reduce the temperature to 150° and dry in a low oven until the meat loses all juices but is still pliable, 1 to 3 hours. Turn once to dry all sides. Remove from the oven and cool completely at room temperature. Meat must be completely dry of juices to store at room temperature.

- Store in tightly sealed containers or plastic bags for up to 1 week. For longer storage, freeze.

MAKES 15 TO 20 STRIPS.

Chocolate meringue pie

2	cups sugar, divided
$^1/_3$	cup cocoa
7	tablespoons cornstarch
$^1/_2$	teaspoon salt, divided
3	eggs, separated
2	cups milk
2	tablespoons butter
2	teaspoons vanilla extract
$^1/_4$	teaspoon cream of tartar
1	baked (9-inch) pie shell (recipe follows)

- In a medium saucepan with a heavy bottom, combine $1^1/_3$ cups sugar, the cocoa, cornstarch, and $^1/_4$ teaspoon salt. Blend well. Beat the egg yolks until light yellow and combine with the milk. Gradually add the milk mixture to the dry ingredients, stirring constantly with a wire whisk.

- Place the saucepan over medium-low heat and cook, stirring constantly with a wooden spoon, until the pudding thickens and comes to a low boil. Remove from heat and stir in the butter and vanilla.

- Pour into the baked pie shell. Preheat the oven to 350°.

- Place the egg whites in a medium bowl. Beat on high speed with electric beaters until foamy. Beating constantly, gradually add $^1/_4$ teaspoon salt, $^2/_3$ cup sugar, and the cream of tartar until the meringue forms stiff peaks.

- Spread the meringue over the chocolate filling, spreading to the edges of the crust and sealing with meringue. Bake for 12 to 15 minutes or just until the peaks are light brown.

MAKES 8 SERVINGS.

*D*ays of our Lives Cast

❧

FRANCES REID as Alice Horton

Mickey Horton	JOHN CLARKE	Austin Reed	AUSTIN PECK
Maggie Horton	SUZANNE ROGERS	Bo Brady	PETER RECKELL
John Black	DRAKE HOGESTYN	Shawn-Douglas Brady	COLLIN O'DONNELL
Caroline Brady	PEGGY McCAY	Jennifer Blake	STEPHANIE CAMERON
Shawn Brady	FRANK PARKER	Abigail Deveraux	PAIGE & RYANNE KETTNER
Abe Carver	JAMES REYNOLDS		
Vivian Alamain	LOUISE SOREL	Kate Roberts	LAUREN KOSLOW
Carrie Brady Reed	CHRISTIE CLARK	Franco Kelly	VICTOR ALFIERI
Samantha Brady	ALISON SWEENEY	Billie Reed	KRISTA ALLEN
Lexie Carver	RENEE JONES	Lynn	MARIE ALISE RECASNER
Lucas Roberts	BRYAN R. DATTILO		
Kristen Blake	EILEEN DAVIDSON	Travis Malloy	BRADEN MATTHEWS
Ivan Marais	IVAN G'VERA	Stefano DiMera	JOSEPH MASCOLO
Laura Horton	JAMIE LYN BAUER	Roman Brady	JOSH TAYLOR
Mike Horton	ROARK CRITCHLOW	Eric Brady	JENSEN ACKLES
Hope Brady	KRISTIAN ALFONSO	Jack Deveraux	MARK VALLEY
Celeste Perrault	TANYA BOYD		STEVE WILDER

With

DEIDRE HALL as Marlena Evans

Simple pastry

Refer to this recipe wherever pie crust is called for.

3 cups sifted all-purpose flour (sift before measuring)
1 teaspoon salt
1¼ cups vegetable shortening (preferably pre-measured
      in sticks)
8 to 10 tablespoons cold water

- Sift together the flour and salt. Blend the shortening and flour together using a pastry blender or two knifes in a cross-cutting motion until the mixture is crumbly.

- Stir in the cold water, adding just enough for the pastry to hold together and form a smooth ball.

- If using a food processor, combine the flour, salt, and shortening in the work bowl. Process on-and-off several times until the mixture is crumbly.

- With the processor motor running, add the liquid in a steady stream and process just until the mixture forms a ball.

- Refrigerate for 1 hour for easier handling. Divide the dough and roll out on a lightly floured board to make pastry for a (9-inch) two-crust pie or two (9-inch) crusts. Roll the dough about 2 inches larger than the diameter of the pan. Drape the crust over the rolling pin and ease it into the pan, fitting it against the bottom and sides. Crust should overlap the edge of the pan about ½ inch. Turn the crust under and shape the edge using your fingers to create a fluted or pleated edge.

- Fill and bake as directed.

- For a baked or "blind" crust, prick the bottom and sides of the crust with a fork. Place in a 450° oven for 10 minutes or just until the crust is set and begins to take on a golden cast. Cool before filling.

JOHNNY ANGEL'S

When you're finished shopping at Ballistix, want to catch a bite after the Salem Cinema, or need some hot chocolate after Salem Place's annual Christmas tree lighting, Johnny Angel's is the place to go. Located in the center of Salem Place, Johnny Angel's opened for business on July 7, 1992. Although it doesn't have the panache of the Penthouse Grill or Chez Vous, there's nowhere else in town that can beat it for a burger, fries, and shake. But if you think it appeals only to the younger set, think again. Johnny Angel's is a favorite with Mrs. H., Maggie Horton, and Marlena Evans. And with Susan Banks's penchant for fried foods, it's no surprise that she and baby Elvis are regulars, too.

M E N U

DOUBLE-DECKER CHEESEBURGER

KILLER CHILI DOG

JOHNNY ANGEL'S CHEESE FRIES

CHOCOLATE SHAKE

VANILLA COLA

CHERRY COLA

Double-decker cheeseburger

2   (¼-pound) hamburger patties
1   teaspoon salt or to taste, divided
½   teaspoon pepper or to taste, divided
2   slices American cheese
4   tablespoons yellow mustard
2   tablespoons pickle relish
1   tablespoon finely chopped or grated onion
1   hamburger bun
Ketchup

- Heat a griddle or large flat skillet over medium-high heat. Place the hamburger patties on the griddle or skillet. Cook until brown on one side. Season with half the salt and pepper. Turn and season the cooked side with the remaining salt and pepper.

- When the hamburger patties are brown and almost ready to remove from the griddle, place a cheese slice on top of each patty. Cook until the cheese softens and begins to melt. Remove from heat and keep warm.

- Pour off the excess grease and place the hamburger buns cut-side down on the griddle or in the skillet. Cook just until light brown around the edges and toasted. The bun should absorb some of the juices from the griddle. Turn and warm the other side of the bun, if desired.

- Remove the toasted buns from the griddle. Combine the mustard, relish, and onion. Spread on the cut side of each bun. Add the hamburger patties, one on top of the other, to the bottom half of the bun. Spread the cut side of the top bun with ketchup, if desired. Add the top bun to the burger.

MAKES 1 SERVING.

Killer chili dog

1   jumbo hot dog
1   hot dog bun
1   tablespoon butter, softened to room temperature
1   tablespoon mustard
$^1/_4$ to $^1/_2$ cup Homemade Chili Sauce (recipe follows)
1   tablespoon finely chopped onion
2   tablespoons finely grated Monterey jack cheese

- Heat a griddle or large skillet over medium-high heat. Place the hot dog on the heated griddle and cook on all sides until patches turn light brown and the skin puffs in places. Meanwhile, spread the cut sides of the bun with the softened butter and place on the hot griddle to toast the buttered side. Cook just until the butter melts and the edges begin to turn golden.

- Remove the bun from the griddle and spread the cut sides with mustard. Place the hot dog in the bun and pour Homemade Chili Sauce over the hot dog. Sprinkle with the chopped onion and cheese.

MAKES 1 CHILI DOG.

Homemade chili sauce

¹⁄₂ pound ground beef
1 tablespoon chili powder
1 cup water
¹⁄₄ cup tomato sauce
1 to 2 teaspoons instant-blend flour
Salt
Pepper

- Crumble the ground beef into a skillet and cook over medium-high heat until the meat is no longer pink. Pour off the grease. Stir the chili powder into the ground beef. Stir to coat the meat well. Stir in the water and ¹⁄₄ cup tomato sauce. Bring to a boil; reduce heat and simmer for about 20 minutes.

- Add more water if needed to maintain a sauce consistency. Stir in 1 to 2 teaspoons instant-blend flour and cook for 5 to 10 minutes longer. Adjust seasoning to taste with salt and pepper.

MAKES ENOUGH FOR 3 TO 4 HOT DOGS.

SUSAN BANKS

In a world of handsome men and beautiful women, Susan Banks is . . . unique—a woman of very distinctive (read "tacky") style. She was introduced to Salem by Stefano DiMera as a surrogate mother for Kristen, but then Susan met John Black and fell in love. When she inadvertently married him in the delivery room at University Hospital, the die was cast and Susan came up with a plan to make John her own. The only problem is, Susan's true love is Elvis, whose name she has tattooed on her ankle, and who she swears is the father of her baby. Susan would like to make Graceland her home—just ask Lisa Marie—but until the real father of her baby is revealed, Susan will be staying put in Salem.

Johnny Angel's cheese fries

$^1/_2$ (2-pound) package frozen French fries
$1^1/_2$ to 2 cups shredded Cheddar cheese
$^1/_2$ cup bottled ranch dressing (optional)

- Cook the French fries in the oven or fry on top of the stove according to package directions. If needed, drain the fries on paper towels.

- Preheat the oven to 450°. Place the cooked French fries on a baking sheet and sprinkle evenly with the cheese. Place in the oven just until the cheese melts, about 3 to 5 minutes. Serve the cheese fries with ranch dressing for dipping, if desired. It is easier to eat these with a fork.

MAKES 2 TO 3 SERVINGS.

Chocolate shake

2   large scoops vanilla ice cream
$^1/_2$ to $^3/_4$ cup cold milk
3 to 4 tablespoons chocolate syrup

- Combine the ice cream, milk, and chocolate syrup in a blender. Blend on high speed until smooth and creamy. Pour into a large, chilled mug.

MAKES 1 SERVING.

Vanilla cola

1   (6-ounce) Coca-Cola in a glass bottle or
        1 (12-ounce) Coca-Cola in a can
Crushed ice
$^1/_2$ to 1 teaspoon vanilla
1   maraschino cherry with stem

- Pour the cola over crushed ice in a chilled glass or frosted mug. Add vanilla to taste. Garnish with the cherry.

MAKES 1 SERVING.

Cherry cola

1   (6-ounce) Coca-Cola in a glass bottle or
        1 (12-ounce) Coca-Cola in can
Crushed ice
$^1/_2$ to 1 teaspoon juice from maraschino cherry jar
1   maraschino cherry with stem

- Pour the cola over crushed ice in a chilled glass or frosted mug. Add cherry juice to taste. Garnish with the cherry.

MAKES 1 SERVING.

Titan Gym Juice Bar

Salem is full of beautiful bodies, and the Titan Gym is where the health-conscious go to maintain them. From Carrie, Sami, Jennifer, Billie, and Hope to Austin, Bo, John, Franco, and Lucas, the Titan Gym is an essential stop during the days of their lives. Whether they're looking to attend an aerobics class, lift some weights, or just work off frustration and tension at the punching bag, fitness fans know this is the place to come. And if looking fabulous isn't reward enough, after the workout there's always a chance for a relaxing sauna or steambath and a high-protein shake or fruit smoothie from the Titan Gym Juice Bar.

MENU

PROTEIN SHAKE

GUILT-FREE PARMESAN POPCORN

FRUIT SMOOTHIE

POWER SALAD

SPROUT AND TUNA SANDWICH

GRILLED CHICKEN SANDWICH WITH ROASTED VEGETABLES

ALL-VEGETABLE SOUP

Protein shake

1   (8-ounce) carton vanilla yogurt
$^1/_2$ frozen banana, cut into 3 pieces
$^1/_2$ cup frozen strawberries or raspberries
$^1/_4$ to $^1/_3$ cup cold skim milk
1   (2-ounce) scoop protein powder or $^1/_4$ cup powdered skim milk
1 to 2 tablespoons honey, or to taste

● Combine the yogurt, frozen fruit, milk, protein powder, and honey in a blender container. Blend until smooth.

MAKES 1 LARGE OR 2 SMALL SHAKES.

Guilt-free Parmesan popcorn

1   (3$^1/_2$-ounce package) plain (no-butter) popcorn
$^1/_2$ cup finely ground fresh Parmesan cheese or to taste
2   teaspoons finely ground pepper

● Cook the popcorn according to the package instructions. Pour the hot popped corn into a large bowl. Sprinkle with Parmesan cheese and pepper. Toss to coat the kernels evenly.

MAKES 4 SERVINGS.

Fruit smoothie

1   cup frozen strawberries, peaches, raspberries, or blueberries (may substitute fresh)
2 to 3 ice cubes (optional)
$^1/_2$ cup cold apple juice
$^1/_4$ cup cold mango juice, pear nectar, or orange juice
$^1/_2$ banana, cut into pieces

● Combine the fruit, juices, and banana in a blender. Blend until smooth. If using fresh instead of frozen fruit, add 2 to 3 ice cubes and process.

MAKES 1 LARGE OR 2 SMALL SMOOTHIES.

Power salad

1   (10-ounce) package fresh spinach
1   (11-ounce) can mandarin orange sections, drained,
        or 1 orange, peeled and divided into sections
$^1/_4$ cup toasted sunflower seeds
$^1/_4$ cup light olive oil
$^1/_8$ cup lemon juice or to taste
$^1/_4$ teaspoon salt or to taste
$^1/_4$ teaspoon pepper or to taste

● Tear the spinach leaves from the stems. Place the spinach leaves in a sink full of cold water, then into a colander to drain. Transfer the spinach to several layers of paper towels to dry completely.

● Place the spinach leaves in a large salad bowl, tearing large leaves into bite-size pieces. Cut the orange sections into bite-size pieces. Toss the orange pieces with the spinach and sunflower seeds.

● Stir together the olive oil, lemon juice, salt, and pepper. Pour over the salad and toss to coat ingredients evenly.

MAKES 4 SERVINGS.

LUCAS ROBERTS

Lucas bopped into town as the boy-toy of a female rock singer and left his military-school career behind. Kate Roberts's youngest son is well on his way to being a master manipulator and worships at the shrine of two of the best—Vivian Alamain and Sami Brady Reed. Although his entrance into Salem was hot and heavy, it was quite a while before Lucas made love again. And when he did, it wasn't with Carrie Brady, the girl of his dreams, but with her sister, Sami. Despite knowing how deceitful Sami can be, the biggest shock for Lucas was her personal betrayal of him—keeping the paternity of his son, Will, secret. That revelation was at least as painful as Lucas's loss of Carrie to Austin Reed. Sami was more than Lucas's partner in crime; he truly cared about her as a friend. But even if he wanted to terminate their relationship, Sami will always be the mother of his child!

Sprout and tuna sandwich

2 slices whole grain bread
1 tablespoon Dijon mustard
$^1/_2$ cup sprouts, your choice
2 to 3 thin slices avocado
1 to 2 thin slices red onion
1 to 2 thin slices tomato
1 (4-ounce) tuna steak, grilled, or $^1/_2$ cup water-pack
 albacore tuna, flaked and drained
1 thin slice non-fat mozzarella cheese

● Spread one side of each piece of bread with mustard. Stack the sprouts, avocado, red onion, and tomato on one piece of bread. If desired, add the grilled tuna steak or flaked tuna. Top with cheese and the second piece of bread.

● *To grill tuna steak:* Brush both sides of the tuna lightly with oil and season generously with salt and pepper. Place under a preheated oven broiler, over hot coals, or in a skillet over medium-high heat. Cook on one side until brown around the edges, 3 to 4 minutes. Turn and cook the other side until browned around the edges, 3 to 4 minutes longer or to the desired degree of doneness.

MAKES 1 SANDWICH.

Grilled chicken sandwich with roasted vegetables

1 or 2 pieces green or red bell pepper, cut flat, about 2x3 inches
1   thick slice tomato
1   thin slice zucchini (sliced lengthwise)
1   thin slice eggplant (optional)
1 to 2 tablespoons olive oil, divided
1   teaspoon dried leaf oregano
1   teaspoon salt or to taste
1/2 teaspoon pepper or to taste
1   boneless, skinless chicken breast half
2   slices Italian bread, toasted

● Preheat the oven broiler. Arrange the vegetables in a single layer in a shallow roasting pan. Sprinkle with the olive oil, oregano, salt, and pepper to taste. Place under the broiler and cook until the vegetables are golden around the edges and easily pierced with a fork.

● Remove the tomato and pepper if they start to get too done. Return the zucchini and eggplant to the oven until softened. Set aside.

● Place a skillet over medium-high heat and add the chicken breast. Cook until golden on both sides and the juices run clear. Season to taste with salt and pepper.

● To assemble the sandwich, brush one side of each piece of toast with olive oil. Stack the chicken breast and roasted vegetables on one piece of toast. Top with the second piece of toast, olive oil-side down.

MAKES 1 SANDWICH.

All-vegetable soup

1   (28-ounce) can tomatoes, undrained
1   cup chopped onion
1   cup chopped celery, including leaves
3 to 4 new potatoes, unpeeled, cut into quarters or eighths
2 to 3 cups water, divided
1   cup sliced zucchini or yellow squash
1   (8-ounce) package frozen corn
1   (8-ounce) package frozen green peas
1   (16-ounce) can white beans, drained
1/2 cup chopped fresh parsley (optional)
2   teaspoons thyme
2   teaspoons salt or to taste
2   teaspoons pepper or to taste
1   teaspoon lemon juice or to taste

● Empty the tomatoes into a large saucepan. Using the back of a spoon, break the tomatoes into pieces. Add the onion, celery, and potatoes. Add 2 cups water. Bring the liquid to a boil over high heat.

● Lower heat and simmer 20 minutes or until the vegetables are easily pierced with a fork.

● Add the squash, corn, green peas, beans, parsley, and thyme. Add more water if a thinner soup is desired. Cook for 10 minutes longer. Season to taste with salt and pepper. Add lemon juice to taste.

MAKES 6 SERVINGS.

BRADY PUB

During all the years that he and wife Caroline owned and operated the Brady Fish Market, Shawn Brady wanted nothing more than to run his own old-fashioned Irish pub. Then two things happened almost simultaneously to make his dream come true: The fish market was vandalized, and John Black inherited his Alamain fortune and gave Shawn the money to open the pub. On September 25, 1992, the Brady Pub opened its doors and has been going strong ever since. On those cold nights when Salemites crave a bowl of hot clam chowder or when they just want to relax in comfortable, familiar surroundings, they head to the Brady Pub for some great grub and TLC.

M E N U

BRADY PUB CLAM CHOWDER

SIRLOIN STEAK SOUP

CATFISH PO'BOY WITH BRADY PUB TARTAR SAUCE

CORNED BEEF AND CABBAGE COOKED IN ALE
WITH MASHED POTATOES

BROWNIE SUNDAES WITH HOMEMADE FUDGE SAUCE

Brady Pub clam chowder

1   cup chopped onion
1   tablespoon vegetable oil or 1 slice bacon, cut into
        confetti-size pieces
2   cups cubed potatoes (about 1 pound russet
        potatoes, peeled)
1   cup water
1   pint (2 cups) fresh clams and their liquor or 2
        (6-ounce) cans minced clams and their juices
3   cups hot milk
2   tablespoons all-purpose flour
2   tablespoons butter, softened
1 1/2 teaspoons salt or to taste
1   teaspoon black pepper or to taste
3 to 4 drops red pepper sauce, or to taste

● In a large saucepan over medium heat, combine the onion and oil or bacon. Cook until the onion is softened, about 5 minutes. Add the potatoes and water. Lower heat to simmer;

cover and cook until the potatoes are easily pierced with a fork, about 15 minutes. Add the clams and their juices along with the hot milk.

- Stir together the flour and butter. Add to the chowder, stirring constantly. Cook over low heat until the mixture thickens slightly. Do not allow to boil. Adjust seasoning to taste with salt, pepper, and red pepper sauce.

MAKES 6 TO 8 SERVINGS.

Sirloin steak soup

1	pound sirloin, cut ¹/₂-inch thick
1	tablespoon vegetable oil
1	cup chopped onion
1	cup chopped celery
1	cup chopped carrots
2	(14¹/₂-ounce) cans beef stock
¹/₄	cup dry red wine (optional)
2	cups cubed potatoes (about 1 pound russet potatoes, peeled)
2	cups (1 8-ounce package) frozen cut green beans

Couples' Favorite Love Songs

Music is an integral part of life, and the sound of a certain song can trigger many wonderful memories. Hum a few bars of any of the following tunes and take a walk down memory lane with your favorite couples from *Days of our Lives.*

Bo and Hope
"Whatever We Imagine"
"Tonight I Celebrate My Love"
"Almost Paradise"
"Holding Out For A Hero"

Bo and Billie
"In Your Eyes"
"I'll Make Love To You"
"Here We Are"

John and Marlena
"In A Perfect World"
"Faithfully"
"Love Won't Let Me Wait"
*"Nothing's Going To Change
My Love For You"*

Jack and Jennifer
"Unbreak My Heart"
"All I Have"
"Wicked Game"

Carrie and Austin
"I Only Have Eyes For You"
"Love Me Tender"
"There's No Easy Way"

Carrie and Mike
"How Do I Live?"

Susan and John
"True Love"
"Mine"

Roman and Marlena
"Up Where We Belong"

1   (8-ounce) package frozen corn
2   tablespoons all-purpose flour
2   tablespoons butter, softened to room temperature
1   teaspoon salt or to taste
1   teaspoon pepper or to taste
1/2 cup grated fresh Parmesan cheese

- Trim the fat from the steak. Cut the sirloin into 2x1-inch strips. Heat the oil in a large saucepan over medium heat. Add the meat and cook, stirring occasionally, until the meat begins to brown. Add the onion, celery, and carrots. Cook until the carrots are easily pierced with a fork, about 8 minutes.

- Add the beef stock, wine, and potatoes. Bring the liquid to a boil. Reduce heat; cover and simmer for 15 minutes. Add the green beans and corn. Bring the liquid to a boil again; reduce heat and cook about 5 more minutes or until vegetables are tender.

- Blend the flour and butter in a small dish. Stirring constantly, add to the saucepan. Cook for about 5 more minutes, until thickened slightly. Season to taste with salt and pepper.

- Garnish each serving with a sprinkling of Parmesan cheese.

MAKES 4 TO 6 SERVINGS.

Catfish po'boy with Brady Pub tartar sauce

To make 4 sandwiches, follow the directions in parentheses.

1   (4) (6-ounce) catfish fillet(s)
1/4 (1) cup milk
1   (2) teaspoon(s) yellow mustard
1/2 (1) cup cornmeal
1   tablespoon (1/3 cup) all-purpose flour
1/4 (1) teaspoon salt
1/4 (1) teaspoon pepper
Oil for frying
Brady Pub Tartar Sauce (recipe follows)
1   (4) soft torpedo (long sandwich) roll(s), split

- Rinse and dry the catfish fillet(s). Combine the milk and mustard. Soak the fillet(s) in the milk for about 10 minutes. Meanwhile, mix together the cornmeal, flour, salt, and pepper.

- After soaking the catfish, shake off the excess liquid and dip in the cornmeal mixture, turning to coat all sides. Set aside on waxed paper for 10 minutes.

- Heat 1 inch of oil for frying in a deep skillet. When the oil is hot (375˚), fry the catfish until golden on all sides, turning once. Cook for 3 to 4 minutes on one side; turn and cook 2 to 3 minutes longer. Drain on paper towels.

- Spread Brady Pub Tartar Sauce generously on the cut sides of the roll(s). Place the catfish fillet(s) between the halves.

MAKES 1 (4) SANDWICH(ES).

Brady Pub tartar sauce

1   cup mayonnaise
1   tablespoon finely chopped fresh parsley
1   tablespoon finely chopped onion
1   tablespoon drained sweet pickle relish
1   tablespoon drained capers, chopped
1 to 2 teaspoons lemon juice

- Combine the mayonnaise, parsley, onion, relish, and capers. Blend well. Adjust flavors with lemon juice to taste.

MAKES 1¹/₃ CUPS.

Corned beef and cabbage cooked in ale with mashed potatoes

1   (3- to 4-pound) corned beef brisket
2 to 3 cups boiling water or as needed
1   (12-ounce) bottle dark beer or ale
1   cup finely chopped parsley
3   cups coarsely shredded cabbage
1   cup coarsely sliced onion
2   pounds (about 4 to 5) russet potatoes, peeled and cut into quarters
2   teaspoons salt or to taste

ROMAN BRADY

The eldest son of Shawn and Caroline Brady's brood has returned from the dead for the second time—or the third, if you count John Black's return as "Roman." Unbeknownst to the real Roman, he's back as the pawn in yet another of Stefano DiMera's schemes. Stefano's interest in the Bradys has shifted from revenge against Roman to capturing Marlena Evans's heart. Roman first met Marlena in 1981, when as a beat cop he was assigned to protect her from the Salem Strangler. What started out as work soon became pleasure as the blue-collar policeman and white-collar psychiatrist managed to overcome their differences and fell in love. Their happiness was short-lived—just long enough to make a dysfunctional family with twins Sami and Eric, and Roman's daughter Carrie (by Anna)—when it appeared in 1984 that Roman had died in a struggle with Stefano. In 1991, Roman returned to Salem to find that John Black had taken over his life and wife. It was with much heartbreak that Roman left Salem again three years later, this time of his own volition, when he learned that John and Marlena had had an affair and that baby Belle was John's daughter, not his. Now Roman is back again, after the ISA had declared him dead, and is hoping to rekindle Marlena's love—since he has never stopped loving her.

$^1/_4$ *cup cream*
$^1/_2$ *teaspoon pepper or to taste*
Bottled horseradish sauce

- Rinse the corned beef to remove the brine. Place in a Dutch oven. Add boiling water to almost cover. Pour the dark beer or ale over the corned beef. Place over low heat; cover and simmer about 1 hour per pound. Add the parsley, cabbage, and onion during the last 15 minutes of cooking.

- Meanwhile, place the potatoes in a large saucepan with just enough water to cover. Add the salt. Bring the liquid to a boil over high heat. Cover, lower heat to simmer, and cook until the potatoes are easily pierced with a fork, about 18 to 20 minutes. Drain the potatoes in a colander and return to the saucepan.

- With a potato masher, coarsely mash the potatoes, using about $^1/_2$ cup of the corned beef cooking liquid to moisten the potatoes just enough to make mashing easy. Use a slotted spoon to remove the cabbage and onion from the corned beef cooking liquid. Stir the onion and cabbage into the potatoes. Stir in the cream. The mixture should be lumpy but moist. Add salt and pepper to taste, if needed. Keep warm.

- Remove the corned beef from the cooking liquid and slice thinly diagonally across the grain. Serve the sliced corned beef over a dollop of the potatoes. Moisten with the corned beef cooking liquid. Garnish with a dollop of horseradish sauce.

**MAKES 4 TO 6 SERVINGS,
WITH LEFTOVER CORNED BEEF.**

Brownie sundaes with homemade hot fudge sauce

2   sticks unsalted butter, melted and cooled slightly
2   cups sugar
2   teaspoons vanilla extract
4   eggs
3/4 cup dark cocoa
1   cup all-purpose flour
1/2 teaspoon baking powder
1/2 teaspoon salt
1   cup chopped walnuts
Homemade Hot Fudge Sauce (recipe follows)
Vanilla ice cream
Bottled marshmallow creme (optional)
Additional chopped walnuts (optional)

● Preheat the oven to 350°. Grease a 13x9-inch baking pan. In a large mixing bowl, combine the melted butter, sugar, and vanilla. Add the eggs, one at a time, beating well with a wooden spoon.

● Add the cocoa and beat until well-blended. Add the flour, baking powder, and salt; blend well. Stir in the walnuts. Pour the batter into the prepared pan. Bake for 30 to 35 minutes or just until the brownies begin to pull way from the sides of the pan. Cool and cut into 3x3-inch bars.

MAKES ABOUT 36 BROWNIES.

To assemble brownie sundaes: Place a scoop of vanilla ice cream on top of a brownie. (If desired, microwave the brownie until warm.) Top with Homemade Hot Fudge Sauce. Drizzle with marshmallow creme and sprinkle with walnuts, if desired.

Homemade hot fudge sauce

8   ounces semisweet chocolate, chopped
1   cup heavy cream

● Place the chopped chocolate and cream in a small saucepan. Cook over low heat, stirring constantly, until the chocolate is melted. Cool until thickened. Reheat gently to serve warm. May be served cold, as well.

MAKES ABOUT 1 1/2 CUPS.

3 HOLIDAYS AND SPECIAL CELEBRATIONS

*H*olidays and special celebrations are part of the ties that bind Salem's families together. During good times and bad, these events provide a sense of stability and continuity in the lives of virtually all of the city's residents. There is great comfort in knowing that no matter how much things may change—or even if Satan comes to town—Christmas will still be observed at Alice Horton's, there will be a Thanksgiving dinner at the Brady Pub, and Kate Roberts will host at least one great party at the Penthouse Grill during the year. Holidays and celebrations are truly special occasions on Days of our Lives because they create lasting memories and bring together the Salem families we love, the ones we hate, and the ones we love to hate.

NEW YEAR'S EVE

Tickets to the New Year's Eve Black-And-White Ball at the Penthouse Grill are hard to come by. But Titan Industries board members and employees such as Kate Roberts, Vivian Alamain, Kristen DiMera, John Black, Carrie and Austin Reed, Lucas Roberts, Hope Brady, Billie Reed, and Franco Kelly are definitely on the "A" list. Crisp white table linens, crystal candle holders, black and white helium balloons, and pure white floral arrangements turn the Penthouse Grill into a slice of heaven where merrymakers can ring in the New Year. Black or white formal attire is de rigueur, and the exquisite menu has a decidedly international flair— Greek, Asian, Latin, and of course bottles of Dom Perignon for that very special midnight toast. But be careful who you're with at midnight because, as Celeste Perrault warned Billie, the man you're with at the stroke of twelve is the man you'll be with for the coming year!

M E N U

COCKTAIL BUFFET

GREEK SKEWERED LAMB
WITH VEGETABLES

MEDITERRANEAN PASTRY TRIANGLES
WITH SPINACH AND FETA CHEESE

GROUND BEEF WRAPPED IN GRAPE LEAVES

SPICY ASIAN BARBECUED RIBS

SALEM HOT WINGS

PIRATE'S SPIKED TEA

MIDNIGHT BREAKFAST

NEW YEAR'S DAY HUEVOS RANCHEROS

Greek skewered lamb with vegetables

2	pounds lean lamb, cut into 1-inch cubes
$1/2$	cup olive oil
$1/2$	cup lemon juice
3	cloves garlic, crushed
1	teaspoon oregano
1	teaspoon black pepper
2	red or green bell peppers, or a combination
2	large red or white onions, or a combination
12	wooden skewers

- Place the lamb in a resealable plastic bag or nonreactive flat dish. Combine the olive oil, lemon juice, garlic, oregano, and black pepper and pour over the lamb. Stir to coat well. Refrigerate at least 1 hour.

- Meanwhile, seed and remove ribs from the peppers. Cut peppers into 1-inch squares. Trim ends from the onions and peel away the thin, papery layers. Cut layers of onions into 1-inch squares, reserving the remaining onions for other use.

- Soak the skewers in water for at least 1 hour.

- Preheat the oven broiler or prepare the fire in the grill. If using charcoal, the coals should be covered with gray ash.

- Drain marinade from the meat. Place the meat on the soaked wooden skewers, alternating pieces of meat with pieces of pepper and onion.

- Place under the broiler or over the prepared coals and cook, turning occasionally, until the meat reaches the desired degree of doneness, preferably medium-rare (pink in the middle), about 10 to 15 minutes. Do not overcook. Serve warm or at room temperature.

MAKES 12 SERVINGS.

Mediterranean pastry triangles with spinach and feta cheese

2   (10-ounce) packages frozen chopped spinach, thawed and squeezed dry
4   eggs
$^1/_4$ pound feta cheese, crumbled
$^1/_4$ pound cream cheese, cut into tiny cubes
$^1/_4$ cup chopped parsley
$^1/_4$ cup chopped fresh dill or 1 tablespoon dried dill
$^1/_2$ teaspoon pepper or to taste
About 1 cup melted, but not hot, butter or approximately 1 cup olive oil
12 to 14 sheets filo (or phyllo) dough, thawed*

- The spinach should be squeezed dry in cheesecloth or pressed against the bottom and sides of a colander to remove as much liquid as possible. The spinach should be crumbly.

- Combine the spinach, eggs, feta, cream cheese, parsley, dill, and pepper in a bowl and mix well to combine ingredients. (Salt probably won't be necessary since the feta is quite salty.)

- Preheat the oven to 350°. Brush a 9x13-inch metal baking pan lightly with melted butter or olive oil. Lay 6 filo sheets in the pan, lightly brushing each with melted butter or olive oil before placing it in the pan. Spread the spinach mixture evenly over the filo sheets. Lay 6 to 8 more filo sheets on top, brushing each one with melted butter or olive oil before placing it over the filling.

- Trim dough to fit the pan or tuck edges down the sides of the pan. Using a sharp knife, cut through the top sheets of filo to make 2-inch squares or diamond shapes. Bake until golden and the filling is set, 45 to 50 minutes. Let rest for 5 to 10 minutes, then cut into squares or diamonds through the bottom layers of dough and serve warm or at room temperature.

MAKES 12 TO 14 SERVINGS.
Thaw filo according to manufacturer's directions. After removing from the package, cover with a damp cloth to prevent the filo from drying and breaking.

Ground beef wrapped in grape leaves

$1/2$ *cup long-grain rice*
36   *bottled grape leaves*
$1/2$ *pound ground beef*
1   *cup chopped onion*
2   *teaspoons finely chopped garlic*
$1/2$ *teaspoon ground cinnamon*
$1/2$ *teaspoon ground allspice*
$1/2$ *cup Toasted Pine Nuts (see recipe on page 29)*
2   *tablespoons chopped fresh mint*
1   *teaspoon salt or to taste*
$1/2$ *teaspoon pepper or to taste*
1   *cup olive oil*
2 to 3 *tablespoons fresh lemon juice*

- Place the rice in a bowl and add enough water to cover. Let stand for 30 minutes; drain.

- Meanwhile, rinse the grape leaves to remove brine. Drain well and remove the stems. Set aside.

- After the rice has soaked, place a large skillet over medium heat. Crumble the ground beef into the pan and cook until the meat is no longer pink. Add the onion and cook until soft, about 10 minutes. Stir in the garlic, cinnamon, and allspice; cook for 3 minutes longer. Place the cooked meat mixture in a large bowl. Add the drained rice, pine nuts, mint, salt, and pepper. Mix well. Adjust seasoning to taste.

- Place a grape leaf smooth-side down on a flat surface. Place a teaspoon or so of the filling near the stem end. Fold the stem over the filling. Next, fold the sides in over the filling and roll the leaf into a cylinder about 1 to $1^1/2$ inches in diameter and $2^1/2$ to 3 inches long. Do not roll too tightly because the rice will expand during cooking. Repeat the process with the remaining leaves.

- Arrange the stuffed grape leaves seam-side down

in a large skillet. Pour the olive oil and lemon juice over the grape leaves. Add enough water to cover by about an inch. Place 1 or 2 plates on top of the grape leaves to weigh them down.

- Bring the liquid to a boil; cover and reduce heat to a simmer. Cook until the rice is tender, about 50 to 55 minutes.

- Uncover the pan and allow the stuffed grape leaves to cool in their cooking liquid.

- When cool enough to handle, transfer to a platter and serve slightly warm or at room temperature.

- Stuffed grape leaves may be refrigerated for up to 3 days before serving.

MAKES 36 SERVINGS.

Spicy Asian barbecued ribs

3 to 4 *pounds baby back ribs*
1   *(8-ounce) bottle soy sauce*
1   *tablespoon sugar*
2   *teaspoons five-spice powder (optional)*
2   *teaspoons garlic seasoning blend*
1   *teaspoon dry mustard*
1   *teaspoon freshly ground black pepper*
Chicken or beef stock for basting
1   *cup barbecue sauce, your favorite brand*
1   *(8-ounce) jar plum jelly*

- Rinse and dry the ribs. Coat the ribs on all sides with soy sauce and place in a resealable plastic bag. Refrigerate for several hours or overnight.

- Combine the sugar, five-spice powder, garlic seasoning blend, dry mustard, black pepper, and paprika, mixing to distribute ingredients evenly. *(continued on page 78)*

MARLENA EVANS

Dr. Marlena Evans is most definitely a woman of her time. In the 1970s, she was a career woman establishing her medical practice. In the '80s, Marlena strove to balance her home and family life with her career. And in the '90s, with her first family grown, she is trying to build a new life with John Black, John's son Brady and their daughter Belle. Marlena first came to Salem in 1976 and was the psychiatrist who helped Mickey and Mike Horton through the crisis that ensued when it was revealed that Mickey's brother Bill was actually Mike's biological father. Since that auspicious start, Marlena has been at the core of numerous key story lines: the Salem Strangler, the Mazatlán adventures, Maison Blanche, demonic possession, and the Paris adventures as Stefano DiMera's Queen of the Night, to name just a few. Her calm demeanor, strong sense of fair play, and high capacity for forgiveness are among the traits that have made Marlena such a popular daytime character. She's not a saint, but Marlena is selfless and always motivated to do what is best for those she loves. Despite her early marriage to Don Craig and subsequent union with Roman Brady (whom she still loves), her true soul mate is John Black, with whom she fell in love when he was believed to be Roman. And therein lies the rub. Marlena's life is plagued by Stefano's obsession with her and the calamities that fixation has caused for Roman, John, her children, and Marlena herself. As a psychiatrist, she is very much aware of daughter Sami's abandonment issues, stepdaughter Carrie's insecurities, son Eric's desire to keep himself apart from his dysfunctional family, and the strife caused by John's and Roman's love for her. But Marlena remains powerless to make things right as long as the nefarious Stefano continues to be the bane of her existence.

- Remove the ribs from the soy sauce, shaking off any excess. Rub or sprinkle about half the seasoning on the ribs, covering the entire surface. Reserve the remaining seasoning for the next time you barbecue. Use on beef or pork.

- Prepare the fire. Coals should be hot but not flaming. Place the ribs 4 to 5 inches above hot coals. Brown on one side, baste with stock, and turn. Brown well.

- Cover the grill and adjust dampers so the fire burns slowly. Grill the ribs until tender and cooked throughout, about 45 minutes. Turn and baste as needed to make sure the ribs don't burn.

- Combine the barbecue sauce and plum jelly in a small saucepan over low heat. Stir and cook just until the jelly melts and the sauce is smooth. About 10 minutes before the ribs are done, brush with the barbecue sauce mixture. Cook for about 5 minutes. Turn the ribs, brush the other side, and cook until the ribs are glazed.

- Cut into serving pieces by slicing through the meat parallel to the ribs. This separates the ribs into individual servings.

MAKES 12 TO 14 SERVINGS.

Salem hot wings

2   pounds chicken wings and drumettes
1   stick butter
1/2 cup Louisiana-style red pepper sauce
2   cups celery and carrot sticks
1   cup bottled Thousand Island dressing

- Preheat the oven to 475°. Arrange the chicken pieces in a single layer on a broiling pan.

- Place in the oven and cook until the chicken pieces are golden and cooked throughout, about 20 to 30 minutes. Turn halfway through the cooking time. To test for doneness, pierce several pieces of chicken at the thickest parts. The juices should run clear.

- Meanwhile, place a large skillet with ovenproof handle over low heat. Add the butter, stirring until melted. Add the red pepper sauce. Stir and cook just until bubbly.

- Place the chicken wings in the skillet, turning to coat well on all sides. If desired, return to the oven to glaze the pieces. Stir occasionally until all pieces are shiny and the edges begin to brown.

- Serve with celery and carrot sticks. Use salad dressing for dipping wings and vegetables.

MAKES 6 SERVINGS.

Pirate's spiked tea

Tea may be served hot or cold.

1   quart freshly brewed tea
3   tablespoons confectioners' sugar
1   quart orange juice
3/4 cup spiced rum or golden rum (optional)
Mint leaves
Thin slices of orange

- To serve hot, brew the tea and stir in the confectioners' sugar. Add the orange juice and heat gently. Place in a thermos or electric coffee pot to keep warm. Add the rum just before serving.

- To serve cold, brew the tea and allow to cool completely. Combine the cooled tea, orange juice, and confectioners' sugar. Stir to dissolve the sugar. Refrigerate for at least 1 hour to chill completely. If desired, add the rum just before serving.

- Serve over ice. Garnish each serving with mint leaves and a thin slice of orange.

MAKES 12 TO 14 SERVINGS.

New Year's Day huevos rancheros

Serve this after midnight when your guests need something substantial for a safe trip home.

³/₄	*cup chopped onion*
1	*tablespoon plus ¹/₄ cup vegetable oil*
2	*fresh jalapeño peppers* or 1 green bell pepper*
1	*clove garlic, finely chopped*
2	*cups chopped very ripe tomato or 1 (16-ounce) can tomatoes, chopped, including juices*

About ¹/₄ cup water (if using fresh tomatoes)

1	*teaspoon salt or to taste*
1	*(8-ounce) can refried beans or 1 (8-ounce) can pinto beans, drained and mashed*
4	*fresh corn tortillas*
4	*whole eggs*

- Place a medium saucepan over medium heat. Add the onion and 1 tablespoon vegetable oil. Cook just until the onion begins to soften, about 5 minutes. Add the peppers and garlic; cook for 2 to 3 minutes longer. Stir in the tomatoes. If using fresh tomatoes, add up to ¹/₄ cup water if the tomatoes don't provide enough juice. If using canned tomatoes, add the tomatoes and just enough of their juice to make a loose salsa.

- Cook until the onion and peppers are soft and the sauce thickens slightly, about 10 minutes. Add the salt. Remove the salsa sauce from heat and allow to cool slightly. Adjust salt to taste. Keep warm.

- Heat the beans in a microwave oven or over low heat and reserve.

- In a small skillet, heat ¹/₄ cup vegetable oil over medium-high heat. Fry the tortillas, one at a time, just until softened, 2 to 3 minutes. Drain on absorbent towels. Spread a thin layer of refried beans over the warm tortillas and keep warm.

- Cook the eggs as desired. Eggs may be scrambled, fried, or poached. Eggs with soft centers (basted or over easy) or poached are the best combination with the salsa.

- When the eggs are cooked, place each on a tortilla spread with beans. Spoon hot salsa ranchera over each.

MAKES 4 SERVINGS.

*Handle fresh jalapeño peppers very carefully. Wear disposable plastic gloves to cut the peppers in half. Scrape out the seeds and ribs, and chop finely. Avoid touching your lips, nose, or eyes if handling peppers with bare hands. Wash your hands thoroughly.

BASTILLE DAY CELEBRATION IN PARIS

When in Rome—er, Paris—do as the Parisians. The summer of 1996 found John Black, Abe and Lexie Carver, Kristen DiMera, Vivian Alamain, and Ivan Marais scouring the streets of the City of Light in search of Marlena Evans and Stefano DiMera. Using Bastille Day as a ploy, Marlena manipulated Stefano into letting her out of the cage in which he had imprisoned her. Then, disguised as Marie Antoinette, Marlena was able to join the throngs of people on the streets celebrating France's national holiday. But Bastille Day (July 14) proved a bittersweet occasion for Marlena, as she was not truly free and her every move was watched by Stefano's People of the Night. As John, Abe, and their French counterpart René grew more frantic in their attempts to locate Marlena, she was accidentally spotted by Vivian and Ivan, who attempted to follow Marlena and Stefano back to his lair. But Vivian's fear of Stefano kept her from alerting John, who found the copy of Marie Antoinette's crown that Stefano had dropped. This inspired John to throw a gala ball, using the real crown as bait to lure the dastardly DiMera into the open. Betrayed by Kristen, however, John failed to do so and wound up with his head in a guillotine.

MENU

SALMON PÂTÉ WITH FRENCH BREAD

LEMON TARRAGON CHICKEN

RATATOUILLE WITH HERBED COUSCOUS

RED-WHITE-AND-BLUE TART

Salmon pâté

³/₄ cup dry white wine
1   teaspoon dried tarragon
1   teaspoon black peppercorns
³/₄ pound fresh, boneless salmon
2   tablespoons olive oil
1   teaspoon finely chopped garlic
¹/₃ pound (about 5 ounces) smoked salmon
2   sticks unsalted butter

2   tablespoons vodka
1 or 2 lemons, sliced very thin, for garnish
¹/₂ cup capers, drained, for garnish
1 or 2 Roma tomatoes, seeded and finely chopped,
         for garnish
¹/₂ cup niçoise (French black) olives, drained,
         for garnish
2   baguettes (long, thin loaves of French bread),
         sliced ¹/₄-inch thick

● In medium saucepan over low heat, combine the white wine, tarragon, and peppercorns. Bring to a slow simmer and cook for 2 to 3 minutes. Cut the fresh salmon into 2 to 3 chunks and carefully slide the salmon pieces into the simmering liquid.

● Allow the liquid to come back to a low, simmering boil. The liquid should be just hot enough for bubbles to break the surface. When the fish begins to appear firm, but is still rosy in color, remove from the cooking liquid with a slotted spoon and allow to cool. Cook the fish no longer than 2 to 3 minutes.

- Raise heat to high and cook away all but 2 to 3 tablespoons of the cooking liquid. Remove from heat and reserve.

- In a small skillet, heat the olive oil over low heat. Add the garlic and cook just until the garlic begins to soften, 2 to 3 minutes. Add the smoked salmon, tossing to coat evenly with olive oil and garlic. Cook 1 to 2 minutes, then drain on paper towels.

- In the work bowl of a food processor, combine the cooled, cooked salmon and the smoked salmon. Process, using pulse or the on-off switch, until finely chopped. Cut the butter into 1-inch pieces and add to the fish along with the reduced cooking liquid and the vodka. Process until quite smooth.

- Pack the fish mixture into a 3-cup round mold or loaf pan. Cover with plastic wrap and chill for 3 to 4 hours. It will keep in the refrigerator for several days. The pâté may also be frozen for up to 1 month.

- To serve, use the tip of a sharp knife to loosen the edges and turn out the pâté onto a plate. Arrange thin slices of lemon around the bottom of the pâté, overlapping the edges. Decorate the top and sides of the pâté with additional lemon slices, capers, and chopped tomato. Arrange the niçoise olives on the pâté and around the edges of the plate. Serve the pâté with thin slices of French bread and a pâté knife for spreading.

MAKES 8 TO 10 SERVINGS.

Lemon tarragon chicken

To double this recipe, follow the directions in parentheses.

1	(2) 3-pound chicken(s)
1/2	(3/4) cup olive oil
1	(2) lemon(s), cut in half
3	(6) cloves garlic, crushed
2	(3) tablespoons dried leaf tarragon
1/4	(1/3) cup lemon juice, or to taste
1	(2) teaspoon(s) salt or to taste
1/2	(1) teaspoon pepper or to taste

- Place the chicken(s) in a resealable plastic bag. In small bowl, combine the olive oil, lemon, garlic, tarragon, and lemon juice. Pour over the chicken(s) and refrigerate for 1 hour.

- Preheat the oven to 375°. Remove the poultry from the marinade, shaking off any excess. Reserve the marinade.

- Season the inside of the chicken(s) with salt and pepper, and rub some into the outside skin. Stuff the lemon halves and garlic cloves into the poultry cavity(ies). Place the chicken(s) breast-side up in a shallow roasting pan. If desired, the bird(s) may be placed on a roasting rack.

- Roast, basting every 20 minutes with the reserved marinade, until tender and the juices run clear when the poultry is pierced in the thickest part of the thigh, about 75 to 90 minutes. Remove from the oven and let rest for 10 minutes. Carve into serving pieces and serve.

MAKES 4 (8) SERVINGS.

Ratatouille with herbed couscous

1/2	cup extra-virgin olive oil, divided
5	teaspoons finely chopped garlic
2	cups (packed) onions, peeled and thinly sliced
2	cups red or green bell peppers (or a combination), seeded and cut into strips
3	cups zucchini, sliced 1/8-inch thick
3	cups eggplant, peeled and cut into 1/2-inch cubes
6	cups fresh tomatoes, chopped, or 2 (35-ounce) cans tomatoes, drained and chopped
1/2	cup chicken broth (optional) as needed
3	tablespoons chopped fresh parsley (2 tablespoons dried)
3	tablespoons chopped fresh basil (1 tablespoon dried)
2	teaspoons salt or to taste
2	teaspoons black pepper or to taste

- Heat 1/4 cup olive oil in a large skillet with high sides or a large saucepan over medium heat. Add the garlic and onions and cook, stirring frequently, over low heat for 6 to 8 minutes or until the onions are softened.

- Stir in the peppers and cook until peppers begin to soften. Add the zucchini and eggplant, along with the additional 1/4 cup olive oil. Cook until the eggplant is soft. Add the tomatoes, stirring well.

- Lower heat to simmer; cover and cook until the vegetables are very soft, about 20 to 30 minutes, stirring occasionally. If more liquid is needed, add chicken broth a tablespoon at a time.

- When the vegetables are very soft, add the parsley, basil, salt, and pepper. Cook for 10 minutes longer, uncovered, allowing the mixture to thicken slightly. Adjust seasoning. Allow to cool to room temperature or refrigerate, covered, overnight.

- Remove from the refrigerator 1 hour before serving or reheat gently, just to take the chill off. If desired, serve over warm Herbed Couscous (recipe follows).

MAKES 8 TO 10 SERVINGS.

Herbed couscous

3 cups chicken stock or water
2 teaspoons salt
2 cups instant couscous
1/2 cup chopped fresh parsley
1/4 cup chopped fresh basil
1/4 cup finely chopped chives
2 tablespoons extra-virgin olive oil

- Bring the chicken stock or water to a boil in a large saucepan. Add the salt. Remove from heat and stir in the couscous. Cover the pan and let stand for 5 minutes.

- Remove the lid and fluff the couscous with a fork. Stir in the parsley, basil, and chives. Just before serving, drizzle with olive oil and toss lightly.

MAKES 8 TO 10 SERVINGS.

Red-white-and-blue tart

The colors of the French revolution are the same as those of the American war of independence: red, white, and blue. This dessert would make a good Fourth of July finale as well. Just keep it refrigerated until serving time.

1 (9-inch) pie shell, unbaked (may use store-bought pastry shell or Simple Pastry; see recipe on page 58)
1/2 cup red currant or red plum jelly
1/2 cup heavy cream, well-chilled
3 tablespoons confectioners' sugar
1/4 cup Grand Marnier or other orange liqueur
1 cup fresh blueberries
1 cup fresh raspberries (or strawberries*)

- Preheat the oven to 450°. Line a tart pan with a removable bottom or a pie plate with the pastry. Place the pie shell in the oven and bake for 10 to 15 minutes until golden. Prick the pastry with a fork if it puffs up. Remove from the oven and cool completely.

- Meanwhile, place the jelly in a small saucepan over low heat. Stirring frequently, cook until the jelly comes to a rapid boil. Cook for 1 to 2 minutes, until the jelly is smooth and shiny. Remove from heat and cool completely.

- No more than 2 hours before serving, place the cream in a small, chilled bowl. Using chilled electric beaters, whip the cream at high speed.

While beating, gradually add the confectioners' sugar. When the cream is nearly stiff enough to hold peaks, add the orange liqueur and continue beating until stiff. Refrigerate.

- Using a small brush or the back of a spoon, lightly coat the bottom and sides of the baked pastry shell with the melted jelly. Spoon in three-fourths of the whipped cream and spread it evenly to the sides. Reserve the remaining whipped cream for garnish. Arrange the blueberries and raspberries or strawberries in a single layer on top of the filling. Alternating concentric circles of blueberries and strawberries make a pretty dessert.

- Reserve a few of the prettiest berries for garnish. Paint the top of the tart with the remaining melted jelly.

- Refrigerate the tart until serving time. Garnish the top, as desired, with dollops of the reserved whipped cream and fresh berries.

MAKES 8 SERVINGS.

John's letter to Marlena

John Black sat in his jail cell in Aremid, awaiting execution for the murder of Tony DiMera. As he reviewed his life, John wrote the following heart-rending note to Marlena Evans, letting her know that he would still love her in paradise.

Dear Marlena:

If you are reading this letter, then I have been executed. No man is without sin, but God knows that I did not kill Tony. I have gone with the faith that death is not the end, but a summons to a new existence, a summons to live with God in paradise.

Of course, I feel that my time has come too soon, but God works in mysterious ways. I leave with few regrets. One is that my children will never know their father. Another is leaving you, Doc.

I know that our life together has been complicated. You've been in love with other men. And I've been in love with other women. But the love we shared was something special, Doc. There never was, and never could be, anyone to fill the special place that you hold in my heart. I love you. I know now I always have. And always will.

John

Horton–Brady Picnic

The annual Horton-Brady picnic began as a casual affair, just two couples—Tom and Alice Horton and Roman and Marlena Evans Brady—getting together for a backyard barbecue. Tom loved to barbecue and was convinced that men make the best chefs. He and Roman greatly respected each other and enjoyed talking about fishing, sports, and the latest happenings in Salem. Marlena and Alice bonded on a different level. Marlena was a career woman, a psychiatrist at University Hospital, where Alice, who had stayed home to raise her children, was a volunteer. Alice was grateful to Marlena for helping son Mickey and his wife Laura overcome emotional traumas. As both families grew, so did the picnic. Roman's daughter Carrie moved in with Roman and Marlena, Marlena gave birth to twins Sami and Eric, and Roman's younger brother Bo returned from the merchant marine. Granddaughters Hope and Jennifer moved in with Tom and Alice, and Bill Horton's son Mike was a frequent visitor. As the picnic became an "official" Horton-Brady celebration, extended family members and friends such as Abe and Lexie Carver were included in the festivities.

M E N U

HORTON FRIED CHICKEN

BRADY BAKED BEANS

KANSAS CORN ON THE COB

GRANDMOTHER HORTON'S FAVORITE SALAD

BRADY OLD-FASHIONED LEMONADE

Horton fried chicken

2 to 3 pounds drumsticks, thighs, and breast halves or
*   chicken tenders**
1   quart water plus 1 tablespoon salt (optional)
1   cup all-purpose flour
1   tablespoon paprika
2   teaspoons salt
2   teaspoons black pepper
1   teaspoon ground sage or poultry seasoning
1 to 2 cups vegetable oil or as needed

- Rinse the chicken. If time allows, soak it in salted water, enough to cover, for an hour. Meanwhile, combine the flour, paprika, salt, pepper, and sage in a resealable plastic bag.

- Place a heavy-bottom skillet with high sides and a lid (preferably cast iron) over medium-high heat. Add ½ inch of oil. Heat until the oil is hot. To test the oil, drop in a small piece of bread. If the oil is hot enough, the bread will hit the oil, rise, float, and turn brown almost immediately.

- Drop the chicken pieces, one at a time, into the flour mixture. Close the bag and shake to coat evenly. Remove the chicken from the flour, shaking off excess, and carefully slide into the hot oil. Repeat until all the chicken is in the pan. Two pans may be needed if time is of the essence. If not, cook the chicken in two batches.

- Fry the chicken over medium-high heat until brown on one side. Turn and fry until the other side browns. Reduce heat to low and simmer for 20 minutes longer. Remove the lid and raise temperature to medium. Cook for 5 to 10 minutes longer or until the chicken is crisp.

- Drain on paper towels and serve at room temperature.

MAKES 8 SERVINGS.

If using chicken tenders, follow the procedure for the bone-in fryer pieces. Soaking isn't necessary for tenders. Rinse, coat with flour, and fry in hot oil, turning until all sides are brown. Drain on paper towels and serve at room temperature.

Brady baked beans

$1/3$	cup sugar
$1/3$	cup firmly packed brown sugar
$1/2$	cup barbecue sauce
$1/4$	cup ketchup
$1/2$	teaspoon salt
1	teaspoon pepper
2	tablespoons molasses
2	teaspoons yellow mustard
3	(16-ounce) cans pork and beans, undrained
$1/2$	cup chopped onion
5	slices bacon, cooked, drained, and crumbled

MICKEY AND MAGGIE HORTON

When Mickey Horton and Maggie Simmons met and fell in love on her farm, Mickey (using the name Marty Hansen) had amnesia and Maggie, who had been crippled in an accident, had led a very sheltered existence. As a result, theirs was an innocent and pure love, which unfortunately was changed by time and circumstances. After regaining his memory, Mickey remained in love with Maggie and was happy to give wife Laura a divorce, but he was devastated to learn that he was sterile and that his son Mike had really been fathered by his brother Bill. As a consequence of his actions after that revelation, Mickey was committed to an asylum. Maggie stood by him during his recovery, and Mickey returned the favor years later when life's pressures led Maggie to drink. They started their own family when Maggie (after using a sperm donor) gave birth to Sarah and the couple won custody of Melissa, who Linda Patterson Phillips had tried to pass off as Mickey's daughter. When it turned out that Neil Curtis was really the sperm donor and not Evan Whyland, as had been thought, the couple again had problems. But time heals, and as the years have passed, the pain of past transgressions has lessened. Having faced their problems together and conquered them, Mickey and Maggie are now one of Salem's happiest and most successful couples.

- Preheat the oven to 350°. Lightly grease a 2½-quart baking dish.

- In a large bowl, combine the sugar, brown sugar, barbecue sauce, ketchup, salt, pepper, molasses, and mustard. Stir to dissolve the sugar. Add the pork and beans, onion, and bacon, mixing well. Pour the beans into the prepared dish. Bake for 1 hour, uncovered, stirring once.

MAKES 10 SERVINGS.

Kansas corn on the cob

5 ears fresh corn on the cob
2 quarts water
1 tablespoon sugar

- Remove the shucks and silk from corn. Trim the ends. Break or cut each ear into 3-inch-long pieces.

- Meanwhile, place the water in a large pot over high heat and bring to a boil. Add the sugar and corn. Cover the pot and bring to a boil again. Turn off heat and let corn stand for 8 to 10 minutes.

- Drain and serve hot with butter, salt, and pepper.

MAKES 10 SERVINGS.

Grandmother Horton's favorite salad

1   (16½-ounce) can pie cherries (water pack, not sweetened)
1   (8-ounce) can crushed pineapple
2   (3-ounce) packages cherry gelatin
1   (12-ounce) can cherry cola (not diet)
1   cup chopped pecans
Lettuce leaves and mayonnaise for garnish (optional)

- Lightly coat a 1½-quart gelatin mold or 9x9-inch casserole with nonstick cooking spray. Set aside.

- Drain the juice from the cherries and pineapple; reserve juice in 2-cup measure. Add just enough water to make 2 cups. Heat the juice and water to boiling. Combine with the gelatin in a medium mixing bowl. Stir until the gelatin dissolves, about 2 to 3 minutes. Pour the cola into the gelatin.

- Place the gelatin mixture in the refrigerator and chill until the gelatin begins to set. The mixture should be thick and somewhat jiggly but not firm. Fold in the drained pineapple, cherries, and pecans. The mixture should be thick enough to suspend the ingredients evenly throughout the gelatin.

- Transfer to the prepared mold or dish. Refrigerate until firm.

Unmold by dipping the bottom of the mold into hot water and inverting onto a serving dish. Loosen the sides with the edge of a knife, if needed. Or cut the gelatin into 16 (2¼-inch) squares and serve on lettuce leaves. Garnish each square with a small dollop of mayonnaise, if desired.

MAKES 10 TO 12 SERVINGS.

Brady old-fashioned lemonade

1 ½ quarts plus ¾ cup water, divided
1 ½ cups sugar
3 cups fresh lemon juice
Thin slices of lemon for garnish

In a small saucepan over high heat, combine ¾ cup water and the sugar. Bring to a boil, stirring frequently. Boil for 1 minute then remove from heat. Stir to completely dissolve the sugar. Allow the mixture to cool.

In a large pitcher, combine the remaining 1½ quarts water (preferably chilled) and the lemon juice. Stir in the sugar syrup. Mix well. Refrigerate until serving time.

Serve over ice. Garnish each serving with a thin slice of lemon.

MAKES 10 SERVINGS.

Halloween Costume Dinner Party

Salem is a great place to be a child, but a holiday such as Halloween seems to bring out the child in everyone. Like mothers and fathers throughout America, parents in this midwestern city are concerned about their children's safety on All Hallows' Eve, which is why they organize special events designed to keep youngsters out of harm's way. For example, Salem Place stages an outdoor festival, complete with Ferris wheel, kissing booth, and cotton candy stand, but the event that captivates kids and adults alike is the charity costume party at the Penthouse Grill. Kate Roberts and Victor Kiriakis host this annual bash, which attracts just about everyone who is anyone in Salem. The decorations are festive, there's an abundance of candy and games for the youngsters, and special prizes are awarded for the evening's best costume. And best of all, the proceeds from the event go to benefit a good cause, the Horton Center. Guys, gals, and ghouls will love the following dishes, which are perfect for a costume dinner party.

MENU

BLOODY MARY CONSOMMÉ
WITH PARMESAN FOCACCIA

ENDIVE WITH PEAR AND GOAT CHEESE
DRIZZLED WITH SHERRY WALNUT DRESSING

CHICKEN BREAST
MASKED WITH GRUYÈRE SAUCE

BLACK AND WHITE RICE

SAMBUCA BAVARIAN
WITH BLACKBERRY COULIS

Bloody Mary consommé with Parmesan focaccia

1	(28-ounce) can Italian tomatoes
2	(10 1/2-ounce) cans beef bouillon
2	cups water
3	tablespoons chopped onion
1	bay leaf
1	stalk celery, cut in pieces
6	black peppercorns
1/2	teaspoon salt or as needed
1/4	cup vodka
3	Roma tomatoes, seeded and chopped fine

- Combine the tomatoes, beef bouillon, water, onion, bay leaf, celery, and peppercorns in a large saucepan over high heat. Bring to a boil; lower heat and simmer, uncovered, for 30 minutes. Strain through a fine-mesh strainer; discard remaining vegetables. Add salt to taste.

- Add the vodka just before serving. Serve immediately in bowls or small cups. Place a sprinkling of chopped tomato in each cup.

MAKES 8 SERVINGS.

Parmesan focaccia

1 or 2 rounds flat bread, such as Boboli
2 to 4 tablespoons olive oil
1 to 2 teaspoons finely chopped garlic
2 to 4 tablespoons grated fresh Parmesan

- Preheat the oven to 425°. Place the flat bread on a baking sheet. Brush lightly with olive oil. Sprinkle with garlic and Parmesan. Place in the oven for about 5 minutes, just until the cheese is melted and the bread is heated throughout.

- Cut into thin wedges and serve with Bloody Mary Consommé (see recipe on page 89).

MAKES 8 TO 12 SERVINGS.

Endive with pear and goat cheese drizzled with sherry walnut dressing

3 to 4 heads Belgian endive (select whitest leaves)
4 ripe pears
1 tablespoon lemon juice
12 to 16 ounces goat cheese
2 teaspoons coarsely cracked black pepper or to taste

- Separate the endive leaves, rinse, and dry. Arrange 4 leaves like spokes on each salad plate, with the points outward. Peel and core the pears. Slice each pear into 8 slices; sprinkle with lemon juice. Place four pear slices on each plate in between the endive leaves.

- Slice the goat cheese into 8 rounds. Place a round of goat cheese in the center of each salad plate, as the axle to the endive and sliced-pear spokes. Drizzle Sherry Walnut Dressing (recipe follows) over the endive leaves and pear slices and sprinkle with black pepper. Serve at room temperature.

MAKES 8 SERVINGS.

Sherry walnut dressing

2 tablespoons sherry vinegar
4 tablespoons walnut oil
2 tablespoons peanut oil (or substitute 6 tablespoons peanut oil for walnut oil)
$1/4$ teaspoon salt or to taste
$1/4$ teaspoon freshly ground white pepper or to taste

- In a jar with a tight-fitting lid, combine the sherry vinegar, walnut oil, peanut oil, salt, and pepper to taste. Shake vigorously to mix. Drizzle over the endive leaves and pear slices. Refrigerate any leftover dressing for use on mixed greens.

MAKES ABOUT 1 CUP.

Chicken breasts masked with Gruyère sauce

1 tablespoon vegetable oil or as needed
8 skinless, boneless chicken breast halves
1 teaspoon salt or to taste
1 teaspoon white pepper or to taste
Gruyère sauce (recipe follows)

- Preheat the oven to 350°. Lightly spray a 13x9-inch ovenproof glass baking dish with vegetable cooking spray.

- Heat a large skillet over medium heat. Add the vegetable oil. Season both sides of the chicken breasts with salt and white pepper to taste. Place in the skillet and cook until golden around the edges on one side, 3 to 5 minutes. Turn and cook the other side for another 3 to 5 minutes or until juices run clear when the fillet is pierced with a fork. Chicken should be cooked throughout, but the breasts should remain as white as possible.

● Transfer the chicken fillets to the prepared baking dish, arranging in a single layer. Pour Gruyère sauce (recipe follows) over the chicken breasts and bake, uncovered, for 30 minutes or until bubbly. Serve with Black and White Rice (recipe follows).

MAKES 8 SERVINGS.

Gruyère sauce

$^1/_2$ stick butter
$^1/_4$ cup all-purpose flour
1 $^3/_4$ cups milk
$^1/_4$ cup dry white wine
1   cup shredded Gruyère (Swiss) cheese

$^1/_2$ cup shredded fresh Parmesan cheese
$^1/_2$ teaspoon salt
$^1/_8$ teaspoon white pepper

● Melt the butter in a medium saucepan over medium heat. Add the flour, stirring until no lumps remain. Cook until bubbly, about 2 minutes. Gradually add the milk and wine, stirring and cooking over low heat until thickened.

● Stir in the Gruyère and Parmesan cheeses. Remove from heat and stir until the cheeses are melted and the sauce is smooth. Taste for seasoning. Add salt, if needed, and white pepper.

MAKES ABOUT 3 CUPS.

Black and white rice

1	cup white rice
1	cup Japonica (black) or wild rice
1	cup chopped white onion, divided
2	teaspoons salt or to taste, divided

- Bring 4 cups water to a boil in 2 medium saucepans, 2 cups in each pan. Add the white rice, 1/2 cup chopped onion, and 1 teaspoon salt to one saucepan. Stir rice and cover. Add the black rice, 1/2 cup chopped onion, and 1 teaspoon salt to the other saucepan. Stir the rice and cover.

- Cook until the liquid is absorbed and the rice is tender, about 20 minutes for white rice, 45 minutes for black rice. Remove from heat and set aside, still covered.

- After allowing the rice to rest for 10 minutes, fluff each batch with a fork and toss together. Cover and keep warm.

- Serve with Chicken Breasts Masked with Gruyère Sauce (see recipe on pages 90 and 91).

MAKES 8 SERVINGS.

Sambuca Bavarian with blackberry coulis

3   cups milk
1   (¹/₄-ounce) envelope unflavored gelatin
¹/₂   cup sugar
3   eggs, separated
¹/₄   teaspoon salt
1   tablespoon sambuca (licorice liqueur) or 1 teaspoon vanilla extract
Fresh blackberries and/or roasted coffee beans for garnish

- Place the milk in the top of a double boiler over, but not in, boiling water. Sprinkle the gelatin and sugar over the milk. Stir until the sugar is dissolved and the milk is hot; remove from heat.

- Beat together the egg yolks and salt. Pour ¹/₂ cup warm milk over the eggs, stirring constantly. Then slowly add the egg mixture to the rest of the milk, stirring constantly. Return to heat and cook until slightly thickened, continuing to stir. Remove from heat and add the sambuca or vanilla. Allow to cool slightly.

- Beat the egg whites until stiff and fold into the warm milk mixture. Pour into eight ¹/₂-cup molds or a 4-cup mold rinsed with cold water. Refrigerate to set the Bavarian.

- Invert the mold or molds onto a serving plate or plates. Puddle Blackberry Coulis (recipe follows) around the bottom and down the sides. Decorate the top and edges of the plate(s) with fresh blackberries and/or dark-roasted coffee beans.

MAKES 8 SERVINGS.

Blackberry coulis

1   (12-ounce) package frozen blackberries
¹/₂   cup sugar
2   tablespoons crème de cassis (currant liqueur)
2   tablespoons lemon juice or to taste

- Thaw the blackberries and place in a blender container along with the sugar, liqueur, and lemon juice. Process until the mixture is smooth.

- Strain the mixture through a fine-mesh strainer to remove the seeds. Chill until ready to serve.

MAKES ABOUT 1¹/₄ CUP.

A Traditional Brady Thanksgiving

Despite all the trials and tribulations of life in Salem, the Brady family has a great deal for which to be thankful: their health, each other, a place to live, and food on the table. That's why each Thanksgiving, before gathering for their family celebration, the Bradys join the Hortons, Robertses, and Carvers as volunteers to prepare and serve Thanksgiving dinner at the shelter. Afterward, the clan gathers at the Brady Pub for a lovely—and lively—holiday repast. The more the merrier is the rule of the day, and Shawn and Caroline can always count on a big turnout, including Roman, John Black (an honorary Brady), Marlena, Carrie and Austin, Sami, Eric, Hope, Bo and Billie, Shawn-Douglas, Belle, Brady, and since her kids are there, Kate Roberts. When they can fly in from Los Angeles, Kim and Kayla and their families also attend. A Brady Thanksgiving dinner wouldn't be complete without a bowl of Shawn's chowder and some oysters in the dressing, but other than that, Caroline serves a traditional Thanksgiving meal.

M E N U

ROAST TURKEY AND MAKE-AHEAD GRAVY

CABERNET CRANBERRY SAUCE

CHESTNUT (AND OYSTER) DRESSING

TWICE-BAKED SWEET POTATOES

LEMON-BUTTER GREEN BEANS

SALEM PUMPKIN PIE

Roast turkey with make-ahead gravy

This is the Bradys' way with turkey at Thanksgiving. The smell of fresh sage as the turkey roasts turns the house into a gustatory celebration of family, fun, and good food.

1 (16- to 18-pound) turkey
2 teaspoons salt or to taste
2 teaspoons pepper or to taste
2 cups fresh sage leaves or 2 tablespoons dried sage
¼ to ½ cup vegetable oil

● Preheat the oven to 325°. Rinse and dry the turkey. Remove the neck and giblet bag from the small cavity in the front, as well as the large body cavity. Use for stock to make Make-ahead Gravy (recipe follows). Season the inside of the turkey cavity with salt and pepper to taste. Use salt sparingly if using a pre-basted turkey. Stuff the cavity of the turkey with the sage leaves or sprinkle dried sage inside the cavity.

● Rub the exterior of the turkey skin generously with vegetable oil and place in a large roasting pan with shallow sides.

● Roast the turkey for 15 to 20 minutes per pound. For the most accurate gauge of doneness, use an instant-read meat thermometer. The temperature should read 180° when the thermometer is inserted in thickest part of the thigh. Juices should run clear when the thigh is pierced at the thickest part, and the leg should move easily at the joint.

MAKES 10 TO 12 SERVINGS, WITH LEFTOVERS FOR SANDWICHES (recipe follows).

Make-ahead gravy

The secret to a Thanksgiving dinner free from last-minute gravy panic is this easy make-ahead turkey gravy.

2 pounds chicken or turkey necks (or a combination) plus contents of bag of giblets inside turkey
1 pound chicken or turkey gizzards and hearts (or a combination) (optional)
$^1/_2$ pound chicken or turkey livers (or a combination) (optional)
8 cups water
1 stick butter
$^1/_2$ cup vegetable oil
1 cup all-purpose flour
3 teaspoons salt or to taste
2 teaspoons pepper or to taste

- Rinse the chicken or turkey necks, contents of the giblet bag, gizzards, and hearts. Place in a large saucepan or stockpot. Cover with 8 cups water. Bring to a boil; reduce heat to simmer. Using a large spoon, skim off foam as it accumulates during cooking.

- Cook until the necks are soft and the gizzards and hearts are tender, 2 to 3 hours.

- Remove from heat and allow to cool. When cool enough to handle, strain the stock into a clean saucepan with lid or into a rigid plastic storage container. Refrigerate to congeal the fat, several hours, up to 2 days. Freeze for longer storage.

- *For gravy with giblets:* Reserve the gizzards and hearts; discard the necks. Chop the gizzards and hearts into $^1/_2$-inch pieces. Refrigerate for up to 2 days. Freeze for longer storage.

- Meanwhile, rinse the livers, if using, and place in a small saucepan with 1 cup water over medium heat. Lower heat and simmer until the livers are cooked throughout, 15 to 20 minutes. Remove from heat and let stand until cool. Drain the livers and discard the liquid.

- Chop the livers into $^1/_4$-inch pieces. Stir the chopped gizzards, hearts, and livers into the finished gravy.

- *For gravy without giblets:* Omit the additional gizzards, hearts, and livers from the stockpot or use them to add flavor to the stock, then feed the gizzards, hearts, necks, and livers to the cat. Animals need to give thanks, too. You can discard the giblets and necks as well.

- To make gravy, lift off the congealed fat from the stock and discard. Heat the stock to liquefy; reserve.

- In a deep saucepan or stockpot, melt the butter over medium heat. Add the oil, then gradually stir in the flour. Cook until the flour is bubbly; reduce heat and cook until the flour turns a golden brown.

- Gradually add the warm stock, stirring with a wire whisk to eliminate lumps. Cook until thickened to the desired consistency, about 20 to 30 minutes. Season to taste with salt and pepper.

- Gravy may be refrigerated for up to 2 days before serving. Reheat to serve. Thin with defatted pan juices from the turkey or with water or stock to the desired consistency.

MAKES 16 SERVINGS.

Leftover turkey and dressing sandwiches

Per sandwich:
1 or 2 slices sandwich bread
Mayonnaise to taste (optional)
2 to 3 slices roast turkey
1 to 2 tablespoons cranberry sauce
$^1/_3$ cup leftover dressing, heated or at room temperature
$^1/_4$ cup leftover gravy, heated

- Spread 1 side of each piece of bread with mayonnaise, if desired.

- Pile turkey, cranberry sauce, dressing, and gravy on one piece of bread. If desired, serve as an open-face sandwich for eating with a knife and fork. Add even more gravy.

- For eating as a pick-up sandwich, top with a second piece of bread. Go easy on the gravy unless you want it running down your arm!

Cabernet cranberry sauce

1 1/2 *cups water*
2 *cups sugar*
1/2 *cup cabernet sauvignon (or other dry red wine)*
4 *cups (1 pound) cranberries*

- Combine the water and sugar in a medium saucepan. Stir until the sugar is dissolved.

- Bring the liquid to a boil over medium-high heat. Let boil for about 5 minutes.

- Add the wine and cranberries. Cook until the berries pop, about 5 minutes. Skim off any foam that accumulates. Cool and refrigerate until serving time.

MAKES 10 TO 12 SERVINGS.

SHAWN AND CAROLINE BRADY

The blue-collar, salt-of-the-earth Bradys came to Salem in 1983. Shawn was a fisherman and owner of the Brady Fish Market. After vandals forced him to close, he opened the Brady Pub. His wife, Caroline, is a woman of very strong faith. That's why it was so shocking when it was discovered in 1985 that she had once had an affair with Victor Kiriakis, who in reality was Bo Brady's father. That revelation explained a great deal to Shawn as he and Bo had always had an adversarial relationship. Despite the fact that Caroline and Victor were truly in love, Caroline did the "right" thing and sacrificed the relationship for the sake of her children. But that wasn't the only sacrifice she made. When daughter Kayla was on trial for murder, Caroline falsely confessed to the crime but was rescued by Victor. Her ties to the Catholic church remained strong, so she was able to assist John Black, Kristen DiMera, and Father Francis when they exorcised Satan from Marlena Evans's body. Shawn and Caroline made peace with the past and now enjoy a relationship that has been made stronger by the tribulations they've endured.

Chestnut (and oyster) dressing

Making this traditional dressing with whole chestnuts can be a chore, but it's worth the trouble.

35 to 40	whole fresh chestnuts (not canned water chestnuts)
1	stick butter, melted
1	cup chopped celery
1/2	cup chopped onion
6	cups dry bread croutons for stuffing
4	tablespoons chopped parsley
2	teaspoons salt, or to taste
1	teaspoon black pepper
1	egg, lightly beaten
1/2	cup cream
2	cups raw oysters and their liquor (optional)

2 to 4 cups warm turkey or chicken stock, or as needed

- Bring a large potful of water to a boil. Meanwhile, using a sharp pointed knife, cut an X into the flat side of each chestnut. When the water boils, add the chestnuts.

- Lower heat and simmer for 20 to 25 minutes. Remove from boiling water with a slotted spoon and drain. Allow to cool enough to handle.

- Peel off the shells and skins. The nut meats should be tender enough to mash. If not, return to boiling water and cook until soft. Drain and mash with a potato masher or place in the work bowl of a food processor and chop, using the on-off switch; reserve.

- In a medium saucepan, melt the butter over medium heat. Add the celery and onion, and cook until the onion is soft, about 5 minutes. Remove from heat and reserve.

- Place the bread croutons in a large mixing bowl. Add the chestnuts, celery, onion, parsley, and salt and pepper to taste. Mix in the egg and cream. If desired, add the oysters and their liquor. Toss to combine well.

- Add just enough warm stock to moisten the ingredients. For a drier dressing, begin with a lesser amount of stock. For a moist dressing, use enough stock to almost immerse the ingredients. The mixture should be thick but not soupy. Adjust seasoning to taste.

- Preheat the oven to 350°. Spray a 9x13-inch baking dish or 2 (1½-quart) baking dishes with vegetable cooking spray. Spoon or pour the dressing into the prepared dishes. Bake for 45 minutes to 1 hour or until golden brown on top and set in the middle.

MAKES 10 TO 12 SERVINGS.

Twice-baked sweet potatoes

6	(about 3 pounds) sweet potatoes
1	cup firmly packed brown sugar, divided
1/2	stick butter
2	tablespoons cognac
1	teaspoon salt or to taste

1 to 2 tablespoons heavy cream

- Preheat the oven to 450°. Lightly butter a 2-quart baking dish. Pierce the sweet potatoes several times with a fork. Place the potatoes directly on the rack in the oven and bake for 1 to 1½ hours or until the potatoes yield easily to the touch. Remove from the oven and allow to cool slightly.

- Using oven mitts to protect your hands, cut the sweet potatoes in half and scoop out the pulp into a large mixing bowl.

- Using a potato masher or electric beaters, mash the sweet potatoes. Reserve 2 tablespoons brown sugar. Mix in the remaining brown sugar, butter, cognac, and salt, beating until the potatoes are smooth. Spoon the sweet potatoes into the prepared baking dish.

- Preheat the oven to 350°. Drizzle heavy cream over the mashed sweet potatoes and sprinkle the remaining 2 tablespoons brown sugar over the top. Bake for 35 to 40 minutes or until golden brown on top.

MAKES 10 TO 12 SERVINGS.

Fascinating Facts about *Days'* Players

Days of our Lives' cast members are a multitalented group whose backgrounds are almost as interesting and colorful as those of the characters they play on NBC's top-rated daytime series.

Krista Allen (Billie Reed) is the beauty in the elevator with Jim Carey in the movie *Liar Liar*.

Kristian Alfonso (Hope Brady) has graced the cover of thirty international magazines, including *Vogue* and *Harper's Bazaar*.

Jamie Lyn Bauer (Laura Horton) won the Junior Miss Phoenix crown in the Junior Miss Pageant in her home state of Arizona.

Tanya Boyd (Celeste Perrault) toured as a backup singer with Anita Baker, Lou Rawls and Natalie Cole.

Stephanie Cameron (Jennifer Blake) loves to mountain climb.

Her love of snowboarding led **Christie Clark** (Carrie Brady Reed) to create her own clothing line, Monkey Wench, which specializes in snowboarding and street wear.

Roark Critchlow found out he had been cast as Mike Horton while at the hospital with his wife, Maria, who was giving birth to their second daughter.

Bryan Dattilo (Lucas Roberts) actually attended Beverly Hills High School.

Eileen Davidson (Kristen Blake) is an avid sports enthusiast whose talents include surfing, tennis, skiing, rollerblading, dancing, and horseback riding.

Deidre Hall (Marlena Evans) was the first performer ever to star in both a daytime and nighttime series, *Days of our Lives* and *Our House*, both for NBC.

Drake Hogestyn considered becoming a dentist when the television show *Seven Brides for Seven Brothers* was canceled. Then he landed the role of John Black on *Days of our Lives*—and the rest is history.

Renee Jones played Salem Police Department secretary Nikki Wade ten years prior to being cast as Lexie Carver.

Lauren Koslow (Kate Roberts) worked as a costume designer before turning to acting full time.

Peggy McCay (Caroline Brady) has received five Emmy Award nominations and holds the unique honor of being the only actor to receive a daytime and a prime-time Emmy nomination in the same year (1987).

Joseph Mascolo (Stefano DiMera) sang a duet with his friend and internationally celebrated supertenor Luciano Pavarotti in the film *Yes, Giorgio*.

Austin Peck (Austin Reed) is an accomplished cartoonist.

Peter Reckell (Bo Brady) garnered *TV Guide's* award for Sexiest Couple in a Nighttime Series (along with Nicollette Sheridan) for his role as Johnny Rourke on *Knots Landing*.

Frances Reid (Alice Horton) had a small role in the star-studded movie *Stage Door*, which featured, among others, Katharine Hepburn, Lucille Ball, Ginger Rogers, and Eve Arden.

James Reynolds (Abe Carver) once worked as a film critic for the *Topeka Daily Capitol*.

Suzanne Rogers (Maggie Horton) was a Radio City Music Hall Rockette.

Louise Sorel (Vivian Alamain) worked as a mime with Jonathan Winters at the Hungry I nitery in San Francisco.

Alison Sweeney was a *Days of our Lives* fan before she was signed to play the role of Sami Brady Reed.

Josh Taylor (Roman Brady) played Jason Bateman's father in the television series *The Hogan Family*.

Lemon–butter green beans

1 (16-ounce) package frozen whole green beans
3 tablespoons unsalted butter
1 tablespoon grated lemon rind (yellow part only)
1 teaspoon salt or to taste
1/2 teaspoon pepper or to taste

- In a medium saucepan, cook the frozen green beans according to the package directions until the beans are easily pierced with a fork, tender but not mushy. Drain the beans and rinse with cold water to stop cooking.

- In a medium saucepan, melt the butter over medium-high heat. When the butter begins to bubble, add the grated lemon rind and salt and pepper to taste.

- Add the beans to the saucepan and toss to coat evenly and heat throughout. Adjust seasoning to taste.

MAKES 8 SERVINGS.

Salem pumpkin pie

No holiday celebration would be the same without this vintage recipe. All of "old Salem" relies on this recipe, which was shared by neighbors over the years. The cardamom makes this pie special.

1 cup canned pumpkin
1 cup evaporated (not sweetened condensed) milk
1 cup firmly packed light brown sugar
3 eggs, lightly beaten
1/4 cup orange juice
1 teaspoon pumpkin pie spice
1/4 teaspoon ground cardamom
1 teaspoon cinnamon
1/2 teaspoon salt
1 (9-inch) pie shell, unbaked (see Simple Pastry recipe on page 58.)

- Preheat the oven to 375°. In a medium bowl, combine the pumpkin, evaporated milk, and sugar, beating on low speed with an electric mixer. Blend until the sugar is dissolved and the mixture is smooth. Stir in the eggs, orange juice, pumpkin pie spice, cardamom, cinnamon, and salt. Mix well.

- Pour the filling into the prepared pie shell. Bake for 50 to 55 minutes or until the tip of a sharp knife inserted in the center comes out clean. Cool on a wire rack. Serve with a dollop of whipped cream, if desired.

MAKES 8 SERVINGS.

HORTON CHRISTMAS TREE PARTY

The Yule season is an especially festive time for the Hortons as the entire family gathers at Alice's home on Christmas Eve for the ritual hanging of the family tree ornaments. Each Horton has a glass ball inscribed with his or her name, and some mysterious things have happened, like the year "Gina's" ornament fell and broke—foreshadowing the discovery that she was really Hope. The family members sing carols, enjoy lots of seasonal food and beverages—including Alice's famous cake doughnuts—and try their best to save room for the big Christmas dinner the next day. The tree decorating party gets into full swing once Dr. Mike Horton returns from University Hospital, where he has carried on the tradition begun by his late grandfather, Tom, of reading *The Christmas Story* to children who are forced to spend the holiday at the facility. (The day this scene is taped is a real family event at *Days of our Lives* as the young "patients" are played by the children of the show's production staff, cast, and crew.)

MENU

HOLIDAY HOT CHOCOLATE

OLD-FASHIONED EGGNOG

ALICE'S FAMOUS CAKE DOUGHNUTS

CUT-OUT SUGAR COOKIES

FRUITCAKE (SEE ENGLISH GROOM'S CAKE RECIPE ON PAGE 115)

MIXED NUT CEREAL SNACK MIX

SUGARED ALMONDS

BEST BROWNIES (SEE RECIPE ON PAGE 72)

Holiday hot chocolate

3   (1-ounce) squares unsweetened chocolate
6   cups milk
1/4 cup sugar
2   teaspoons ground cinnamon, omit if using peppermint sticks
1/4 teaspoon salt
2   teaspoons vanilla extract
1   cup brandy or bourbon or to taste (optional)
6   peppermint sticks (optional)

● Using a sharp knife, break up the chocolate squares into smaller pieces.

● In a medium saucepan, combine the chocolate, milk, sugar, cinnamon (if using), and salt. Heat and stir until the chocolate melts and the milk is very hot. Do not allow to boil. Add the vanilla and spirits, if desired. Beat until frothy with a rotary beater or with an electric mixer on low speed.

● Pour into mugs. Garnish each with a peppermint stick, if desired.

MAKES 6 (8-OUNCE) SERVINGS.

Old-fashioned eggnog

Although it is called "old-fashioned," this eggnog has been updated to reflect contemporary food safety concerns. The most traditional preparation —with a dozen raw eggs—has fallen out of favor in recent years because of concerns about salmonella bacteria. This version, adapted to use a boiled custard instead of raw eggs, keeps the Horton tradition alive in a tasty and authentic way.

$^1/_3$ cup plus 3 tablespoons sugar, divided
2   eggs, separated
$^1/_4$ teaspoon salt
4   cups milk
2   teaspoons vanilla extract
1   cup dark rum or brandy (optional)
$^1/_2$ cup whipping cream
Ground nutmeg

- In large saucepan, combine $^1/_3$ cup sugar and the egg yolks. Beat until smooth and light yellow in color. Add the salt and stir in the milk. Cook over medium heat, stirring constantly, until the mixture thickens enough to coat the back of a spoon.

- Remove from heat and stir in the vanilla. Transfer the custard to a bowl or pitcher. Stir in the rum or brandy, if desired. Place a layer of plastic wrap directly on the custard. Refrigerate to cool completely, 3 to 4 hours.

- Just before serving, whip the cream until soft peaks form. Pour the chilled eggnog into a chilled punch bowl and gently fold in the whipped cream. Sprinkle with nutmeg.

MAKES 6 TO 8 SERVINGS.

Alice's famous cake doughnuts

2   eggs
1   cup sugar
1   cup milk
5   tablespoons melted shortening
1   teaspoon vanilla extract
4   cups all-purpose flour, sifted before measuring
4   teaspoons baking powder
$^1/_2$ teaspoon salt
1   stick butter, melted
Cinnamon Sugar (recipe follows)

- In a large bowl, beat the eggs until foamy. Gradually add the sugar, beating constantly. Stir in the milk, shortening, and vanilla.

- Sift together the flour, baking powder, and salt. Add to the dry ingredients, mixing well. Cover and chill the dough for 30 minutes to 1 hour for easier handling.

- Preheat the oven to 450°. Spray a baking sheet with vegetable cooking spray.

- Roll out or pat the dough on a lightly floured board to a ½-inch thickness. Cut with a doughnut cutter. Place the doughnuts and holes on the baking sheet, about 1 inch apart. Bake for 10 to 15 minutes or until golden brown.

- Brush each doughnut and doughnut hole with melted butter and roll in Cinnamon Sugar to coat all sides.

MAKES ABOUT 36 DOUGHNUTS.

Cinnamon sugar

1   *cup sugar*
1   *teaspoon cinnamon*

- In a small bowl, combine the sugar and cinnamon, blending well.

ALICE HORTON

The matriarch of the Horton family, Alice Horton has been a part of the lives of Salem watchers since Days of our Lives *was first broadcast on November 8, 1965. She has been a successful wife, mother, grandmother, great-grandmother, hospital volunteer, fund raiser, restaurateur, youth advisor, and jailbreaker. Now that her longtime husband, Tom, is gone, Alice is the glue that holds together the lives of the Horton clan. Mrs. H is who granddaughters Jennifer and Hope, and Bo Brady turn to for advice. Alice, according to* Days *head writer Jim Reilly, is "the truth teller." When Hope's identity was in doubt, Alice knew who she was for certain. When Jennifer married Peter Blake, Alice was sure that Jack Deveraux was really Jen's true love. What makes Alice so popular after thirty-two years is her genuine interest in the Hortons and the Bradys, her penchant for offering guidance without actually expecting her family to follow it, and her uncanny ability never to say "I told you so!"*

Cut-out sugar cookies

Decorating these sugar cookies is as much a part of Christmas as decorating the tree. These simple sugar cookies are easy to make as pressed cookies, or you may want to roll them and then cut into holiday shapes.

$^1/_2$ cup vegetable shortening
1   cup sugar
1   egg, lightly beaten
1   teaspoon vanilla extract
$^1/_4$ cup milk
2 $^1/_2$ cups all-purpose flour
2   teaspoons baking powder
$^1/_4$ teaspoon salt

- Preheat the oven to 375°. In a medium bowl, combine the shortening and the sugar, beating at high speed with an electric mixer. The mixture should be light and fluffy. Add the egg, vanilla, and milk.

- Sift together the flour, baking powder, and salt. Repeat the sifting process, then blend the sifted ingredients into the egg and sugar mixture.

- Chill the dough for 1 to 2 hours for easier handling.

- *Pressed cookies:* Roll the dough into 1-inch balls. Place the balls on an ungreased cookie sheet 2 inches apart. Press each ball with the bottom of a glass that has been dipped in sugar until the

dough is about ¼-inch thick. Sprinkle lightly with ground nutmeg or cinnamon. If desired, place an almond or walnut half in the center of each or sprinkle with other holiday cookie decorations. Bake for 8 to 10 minutes or until light golden around the edges. Remove from the oven and allow to cool until the cookies begin to firm up. Remove to a rack to cool completely.

● *Cut-out cookies*: Break off one-third to one-fourth of the dough, returning the rest to the refrigerator. Place on a lightly floured board and gently roll out to a ¼-inch thickness.

● Using holiday cutters, cut the cookies into desired shapes. Using a spatula, carefully transfer to ungreased baking sheet. Decorate as desired with sprinkles or other holiday decorations. Bake for 8 to 10 minutes or until lightly golden around the edges. Remove from oven and allow to cool until cookies begin to firm up. Remove to a rack to cool completely.

● Decorate as desired with frosting (recipe follows), commercial icing, colored sugar, or other cookie decorations.

MAKES 2½ TO 3 DOZEN COOKIES.

Frosting for cookies

½   cup confectioners' sugar
2   teaspoons unsalted butter, softened to
        room temperature
2   teaspoons milk
Food coloring as desired

● In a small bowl, combine the sugar, butter, and milk. Beat with an electric mixer at medium speed until smooth. Separate the frosting into batches. Add a few drops of food coloring to each, as desired. Pipe or spread one or more colors onto the completely cooled cookies. After decorating, let stand until the frosting is set. Store in loosely covered container.

Mixed nut cereal snack mix

1   *(15-ounce) package round oat cereal*
1   *(12-ounce) package crispy waffle rice cereal*
1   *(12-ounce package crispy waffle corn cereal*
1   *(9-ounce) package pretzel sticks*
1   *cup almond halves*
1   *cup pecan halves*
1   *cup cashews*
1   *cup peanuts*
4   *sticks butter*
½   *cup Worcestershire sauce or to taste*
2   *teaspoons garlic salt or to taste*
A *few drops red pepper sauce to taste (optional)*

● In large bowl, toss together the cereals, pretzels, and nuts.

● Preheat the oven to 325°. Place the butter in a large roasting pan with sides. Melt the butter in the oven. When the butter melts, remove the pan from the oven and stir in the Worcestershire sauce, garlic salt, and red pepper sauce, if desired.

● Stir the nut-cereal mixture into the melted butter, tossing to coat each piece. Place in the oven and bake for 30 to 40 minutes or until the cereal is golden brown and crisp.

MAKES 1½ QUARTS.

Sugared almonds

1   cup sugar
$1/8$ teaspoon cream of tartar
$1/4$ cup boiling water
$1 1/2$ cups blanched whole almonds
$1/2$ teaspoon vanilla extract

● In a small saucepan over medium heat, combine the sugar, cream of tartar, and boiling

water. Stirring constantly, cook until boiling. Cook until a candy thermometer reaches 240° (soft-ball stage).

● Remove from heat and stir in the almonds. Allow to cool a few minutes. Add the vanilla and stir until the almonds are thoroughly coated. Pour the almonds onto waxed paper and separate.

MAKES 2 CUPS.

4 WEDDINGS

Any television series that can maintain a large and loyal following for more than three decades is definitely doing something right. One of the primary reasons that Days of our Lives continues to be so popular with daytime viewers is the show's ability to portray extraordinary love stories—especially those that involve a first love. Each wedding in this chapter is, in one way or another, representative of that theme. In 1985, when Bo Brady and Hope Williams married, nearly everyone believed their love would be eternal. And despite a host of unsettling problems, the one sure thing in their lives is that their love for each other has not died. After three and a half tempestuous years, love finally triumphed for star-crossed lovers Carrie Brady and Austin Reed, who made it to the altar in September 1997. Billie Reed and Sami Brady also married their first loves, but both weddings were shams and the love the young brides felt for their respective grooms was not reciprocated. Three of the four weddings depicted here were international affairs—Bo and Hope exchanged their vows in England, Sami and Austin were wed in Paris, and Bo and Billie were married in Rome—while Austin and Carrie tied the nuptial knot in Salem.

BO AND HOPE'S ENGLISH WEDDING TEA

Bo Brady and Hope Williams saw each other for the first time as young adults at Roman Brady's home. Hope had a crush on Roman, but it wasn't long before his younger brother became the focus of her attention. Hope was beautiful, slightly spoiled, and had led a decidedly sheltered life. Bo had just returned from the merchant marine, was rough around the edges, and a great deal more worldly. The sweethearts made love for the first time in New Orleans and planned to marry. Then, Hope became entangled in an ISA investigation. She was the only person to have seen the face of the Dragon, an anti-monarchist who had killed Prince Nicholas and was plotting to kill Lady Joanna. Bo and Hope finally captured the terrorist in the Tower of London, and Lady Joanna was so grateful that she gave the couple the wedding of their dreams at St. Mary's Church in the Cotswold. The bride and groom were delayed and ultimately had to steal a horse to get to the church on time. The ceremony was spectacular , but Bo was arrested afterward and the newlyweds were compelled to spend their wedding night in an English jail.

MENU

❧

SMOKED SALMON CANAPÉS

BABY POTATOES STUFFED WITH CAVIAR AND SOUR CREAM

TEA SANDWICHES

ROAST BEEF WITH HORSERADISH CREAM

LEMON WEDDING CAKE

ENGLISH GROOM'S CAKE

RASPBERRY (OR APRICOT) FILLED BUTTER COOKIES

GINGERED CITRUS PUNCH

Smoked salmon canapés

2   sticks salted butter, softened to room temperature
2 to 3 tablespoons milk
2   tablespoons minced fresh dill
3   (16-ounce) packages sliced party breads
3   (12-ounce) packages thinly sliced smoked salmon
1   small red onion
1   small white onion
1   (3¼-ounce) bottle of large capers, drained
Small sprigs of fresh dill

- Beat the softened butter with an electric mixer until fluffy. Add just enough milk to make a creamy, spreadable consistency. Blend in the minced fresh dill. Spread one side of 36 slices of bread. Refrigerate until ready to use.

- Cut the salmon into thin strips. Slice the onions as thinly as possible and make sure the capers are dry. Rinse, separate, and dry small sprigs of fresh dill for garnish.

- *To assemble sandwiches:* Place a small mound of salmon strips on the spread-side of the bread. Press gently so the salmon will adhere. Garnish with a thin slice of red onion, white onion, a couple of capers, or a sprig of fresh dill. If the garnish slides off easily, use a bit of butter on the underside to "cement" it to the canapé.

- If desired, trim the crusts to make uniform shapes. For other shapes, trim the bread after spreading but before assembling the sandwiches.

MAKES 36 CANAPÉS.

BO BRADY

Bo Brady has all the charm of the Irish, even though Greek tycoon Victor Kiriakis is his biological father. Raised by Caroline and Shawn Brady, Bo was a bit of a rogue in his younger days. On his return to Salem from the merchant marine, he encountered former childhood friend Hope Williams. Although Bo repeatedly denied his attraction to uptown girl Hope, he finally proclaimed his love for her and swept her away on the day she was to marry shady Salem District Attorney Larry Welch. When Welch's henchmen threatened to harm the Brady family unless she went through with the marriage, Hope wed Larry. She eventually exposed Larry's illicit dealings and declared her love for Bo. Hope and Bo exchanged marital vows in a beautiful ceremony in England, but they were not to be happy for long. Hope was believed to have been killed in an accident caused by Ernesto Toscano, and Bo was inconsolable but finally pulled his life together to raise their son, Shawn-Douglas. When Carly Manning entered his life, it appeared that Bo had once again found love. But it was Billie Reed who actually got Bo to walk down the aisle for a second time—and a third. But when it was discovered that Hope had not died, Bo faced a major dilemma in deciding which woman was his true love. Although he was forced to remarry Billie, Bo hopes to again make Hope his wife and reunite his family. He'd also like to rebuild his boat, the Fancy Face, and continue solving crimes as a member of the Salem Police Department.

Weddings

Baby potatoes stuffed with caviar and sour cream

These caviar-filled treats will fairly explode in your mouth.

48   new (red) potatoes, all about the same size, no
        bigger than a Ping-Pong ball
Salt to taste
Pepper to taste
1   (8-ounce) carton sour cream
1   (2-ounce) jar of caviar, red, black, or golden
        (or some of each)

- Scrub and rinse the potatoes. Do not peel. Place in a large saucepan with enough water to cover. Over high heat, bring the water to a boil and cook until the potatoes are soft but not falling apart, about 12 minutes. Potatoes are done if they can be easily pierced with a fork.

- Drain the water and allow the potatoes to cool completely. Refrigerate if desired.

- When the potatoes are cool, use a small melon baller to scoop out the middles. Lightly sprinkle the inside of each potato with salt and pepper. Place just enough sour cream in each to fill the scoop, about 1 teaspoon.

- Sprinkle the sour cream filling in each potato with caviar. Select red, black, or golden, or for a variety of color, use some of each. Refrigerate until ready to serve.

MAKES 4 DOZEN POTATOES.

Tea sandwiches

2   cucumbers, unpeeled
4   Roma tomatoes
1¹/₂ teaspoons salt or to taste, divided
1   bunch watercress
2   (6-ounce) packages cream cheese, softened to
        room temperature
2   tablespoons finely grated white onion
¹/₈ teaspoon hot pepper sauce
1 to 2 tablespoons mayonnaise or to taste
4   (16-ounce) packages sliced party breads

- Slice the cucumbers and tomatoes as thinly as possible. Place on absorbent paper towels to drain. Very lightly sprinkle with ¹/₂ teaspoon salt. Cover with another layer of paper towels. Rinse and dry the watercress.

- Meanwhile, blend the cream cheese, onion, 1 teaspoon salt, hot pepper sauce, and mayonnaise. Use only enough mayonnaise to achieve a spreadable consistency. Adjust

seasoning with salt and hot pepper sauce as desired.

- Spread one side of each slice of bread with the cream cheese mixture. Apply the cream cheese in a thin, even layer all the way to the edges of each slice.

- *To assemble sandwiches:* Place a thin slice of cucumber, tomato, or a few watercress leaves on a piece of bread, spread-side up. Top with another slice of bread, spread-side down. Press to seal. Cut off the crusts, if desired.

- For smaller pieces, cut the sandwiches in half diagonally.

MAKES 48 SANDWICHES.

Roast beef with horseradish cream

1   (4- to 5-pound) top round roast or chuck tender
2   teaspoons salt or to taste
2   teaspoons cracked black pepper or to taste
40 small, round rolls (white, whole grain,
       pumpernickel, or a combination)
Soft butter (optional)

● Preheat the oven to 325°. Sprinkle the roast on all sides with salt and pepper to taste and place in a shallow roasting pan.

● Roast for about 25 minutes per pound for medium-rare; 30 minutes per pound for medium-well.

● Remove the meat from the oven and allow to cool to room temperature. Chill until ready to prepare the sandwiches.

● When ready to serve, slice the meat into very thin slices, approximately the size of the rolls.

● Slit the rolls horizontally. If desired, spread the cut sides of each roll lightly with the butter. This will help prevent the bread from becoming soggy. Place 1 or 2 slices of meat between the halves of each roll.

● Serve the sandwiches on a tray with a serving dish of Horseradish Cream (recipe follows).

MAKES 40 SANDWICHES.

Horseradish cream

1   cup heavy cream
1/2 teaspoon salt
1/3 cup well-drained white horseradish
1   tablespoon prepared mustard

● In a medium bowl, whip the cream until stiff peaks form. Add the salt while beating. Fold in the horseradish and mustard. The cream will hold in the refrigerator, covered, for up to 3 hours.

Lemon wedding cake

This recipe makes a 2-layer cake with lemon filling and lemon buttercream icing. The pastry chefs worked for three days on the one for Bo and Hope's wedding, but the cake below will take only about half a day of your time.

Layers
1 1/2 sticks unsalted butter, softened
1 3/4 cups minus 1 tablespoon sugar
2 3/4 cups all-purpose flour, sift before measuring
3/4 teaspoon salt
2 1/2 teaspoons baking powder
1   cup plus 2 tablespoons water
1   teaspoon lemon extract
4   egg whites, at room temperature

● Preheat the oven to 375°. Grease and flour 2 (9-inch) cake pans.

● In a large mixing bowl, beat together the butter and sugar until light and fluffy. In another medium bowl, sift together the flour, salt, and baking powder.

● Add the dry ingredients to the creamed mixture alternately with the water, mixing well after each addition. Begin and end with dry ingredients. Stir in the lemon extract.

- Place the egg whites in a medium mixing bowl and beat until the whites hold stiff peaks. Using a rubber spatula, gently fold the egg whites into the batter.

- Pour equal amounts of the batter into each pan. Bake for 20 to 30 minutes or until done. Test for doneness by inserting a tester in the center of each pan. If the tester comes out clean, the cake is done. Do not overbake.

- Remove the cakes from the oven and allow to cool for 10 minutes. Carefully, turn out the layers onto racks and cool completely.

Filling

1¼ tablespoons cornstarch
⅓ cup sugar
⅛ teaspoon salt
¼ cup water
2 tablespoons lemon juice
¼ teaspoon grated lemon rind
2 teaspoons butter
2 lightly beaten egg yolks
1 whole lemon (optional)

———

- In the top of a double-boiler over—not in—boiling water, combine the cornstarch, sugar, and salt. Gradually, stir in the water, lemon juice, lemon rind, and butter. Cook for about 5 minutes, stirring constantly. Cover and cook for about 7 to 10 minutes longer without stirring.

- Remove from heat and gently stir in the egg yolks. Return to heat and cook for about 2 minutes longer, stirring constantly. Remove from heat and allow to cool, stirring occasionally.

- Slice the lemon into paper-thin slices and reserve.

Icing

1 stick butter, softened to room temperature
¼ teaspoon salt
2½ cups confectioners' sugar, sifted before measuring
3 to 4 tablespoons lemon juice
2 teaspoons grated lemon rind
1 teaspoon vanilla extract

———

- In a medium bowl, beat the butter until light and fluffy. Add the salt and sugar gradually, beating constantly. Add the lemon juice as needed to achieve a spreadable consistency. Stir in the lemon rind and vanilla.

- *To assemble the cake:* Place 1 cooled layer, flat-side up, on a cake plate or serving platter. Spread the filling about ¼-inch thick on top of the bottom layer about 1 inch from the edges. Some filling may be left over. Refrigerate and use within 2 to 3 days as a spread for toast or pancakes.

- If using lemon slices, arrange the slices in circles, starting at the center of the layer. Edges should barely overlap. Spread a bit more filling over the slices to glaze them.

- Place the second layer, flat-side down, on top of the filling. If needed to secure layers, insert toothpicks at several points along the perimeter of the bottom layer. Place the second layer on top of the toothpicks. Remember to watch for the toothpicks when slicing, and be sure to remove them before serving.

- Spread the sides of the cake with icing. Swirl the icing on top of the cake. Use icing to seal the cake at the bottom and where the layers meet.

- If desired, dip paper-thin slices of lemon into the glaze and use to decorate the top of the cake. Or drizzle some of the filling on top of the cake.

MAKES 12 TO 16 SERVINGS.

SOAP OPERA DIGEST AWARDS WON BY *DAYS OF OUR LIVES*

First Annual Awards Presentation (1984)

Outstanding Show:	*Days of our Lives*
Outstanding Actress:	Deidre Hall (Marlena Evans)
Outstanding Actor:	Peter Reckell (Bo Brady)
Outstanding Supporting Actress:	Lisa Trusel (Melissa Phillips Anderson)
Outstanding Supporting Actor:	John de Lancie (Eugene Bradford)
Outstanding Female Newcomer:	Kristian Alfonso (Hope Williams)
Outstanding Male Newcomer:	Michael Leon (Pete Jannings)
Outstanding Actress/Mature Role:	Frances Reid (Alice Horton)
Outstanding Actor/mature Role:	Macdonald Carey (Tom Horton)
Outstanding Villain:	Joseph Mascolo (Stefano DiMera)
Outstanding Youth Actress:	Andrea Barber (Carrie Brady)

Second Annual Awards Presentation (1985)

Outstanding Show:	*Days of our Lives*
Outstanding Actress:	Deidre Hall (Marlena Evans)
Outstanding Actor:	Peter Reckell (Bo Brady)
Outstanding Supporting Actress:	Arleen Sorkin (Calliope Jones Bradford)
Outstanding Supporting Actor:	John de Lancie (Eugene Bradford)
Outstanding Female Newcomer:	Arleen Sorkin (Calliope Jones)
Outstanding Male Newcomer:	Charles Shaughnessy (Shane Donovan)
Outstanding Actress/Mature Role:	Frances Reid (Alice Horton)
Outstanding Actor/Mature Role:	Macdonald Carey (Tom Horton)
Outstanding Villainess:	Cheryl-Ann Wilson (Megan Hathaway)
Outstanding Villain:	Joseph Mascolo (Stefano DiMera)
Outstanding Youth Actress:	Andrea Barber (Carrie Brady)
Outstanding Youth Actor:	Brian Autenrieth (Zach Parker)

Third Annual Awards Presentation (1986)

Outstanding Show:	*Days of our Lives*
Outstanding Actress:	Patsy Pease (Kimberly Brady Donovan)
Outstanding Actor:	John Aniston (Victor Kiriakis)
Outstanding Supporting Actor:	Stephen Nichols (Stephen "Patch" Johnson)
Outstanding Younger Leading Actor:	Peter Reckell (Bo Brady)
Outstanding Villain:	John Aniston (Victor Kiriakis)
Outstanding Comic Performer:	Arleen Sorkin (Calliope Jones Bradford)
Favorite Super Couple:	Charles Shaughnessy and Patsy Pease (Shane and Kimberly)

Fourth Annual Awards Presentation (1988)

Outstanding Show:	*Days of our Lives*
Outstanding Actor:	Stephen Nichols (Stephen "Patch" Johnson)
Outstanding Comic Actress:	Arleen Sorkin (Calliope Jones Bradford)
Outstanding Super Couple:	Charles Shaughnessy and Patsy Pease (Shane and Kimberly)

Fifth Annual Awards Presentation (1989)

Outstanding Show:	*Days of our Lives*
Outstanding Hero:	Stephen Nichols (Stephen "Patch" Johnson)
Favorite Super Couple:	Stephen Nichols and Mary Beth Evans (Patch Johnson and Kayla Brady)

Sixth Annual Awards Presentation (1990)

Outstanding Villainess:	Jane Elliot (Anjelica Deveraux Curtis)

Seventh Annual Awards Presentation (1991)

Outstanding Show:	*Days of our Lives*
Outstanding Super Couple:	Matthew Ashford and Melissa Reeves (Jack and Jennifer)

Eighth Annual Awards Presentation (1992)

Outstanding Show:	*Days of our Lives*
Outstanding Comic Performer:	Robert Mailhouse (Brian Scofield)
Best Wedding:	Matthew Ashford and Melissa Reeves (Jack and Jennifer)

Prime Time:

Best Love Story, Daytime or Prime Time:	Matthew Ashford and Melissa Reeves (Jack and Jennifer)

Ninth Annual Awards Presentation (1993)

Favorite Show:	*Days of our Lives*
Outstanding Supporting Actor:	Richard Biggs (Marcus Hunter)
Outstanding Comic Performance:	Matthew Ashford (Jack Deveraux)
Hottest Female Star:	Crystal Chappell (Carly Manning)
Favorite Song:	"One Dream"

Tenth Annual Awards Presentation (1994)

Favorite Show:	*Days of our Lives*
Male Newcomer:	Patrick Muldoon (Austin Reed)
Outstanding Villain/Villainess:	Louise Sorel (Vivian Alamain)
Outstanding Child Actor:	Scott Groff (Shawn-Douglas Brady)
Outstanding Supporting Actress:	Deborah Adair (Kate Roberts)
Outstanding Female Newcomer:	Lisa Rinna (Billie Reed)
Musical Achievement:	*Days of our Lives*
Hottest Female Star:	Melissa Reeves (Jennifer Deveraux)
Hottest Male Star:	Drake Hogestyn (John Black)
Outstanding Storyline:	"Who Fathered Marlena's Baby?"
Outstanding Lead Actor:	Robert Kelker-Kelly (Bo Brady)

Eleventh Annual Awards Presentation (1995)

Favorite Show:	*Days of our Lives*
Hottest Male Star:	Drake Hogestyn (John Black)
Outstanding Lead Actress:	Deidre Hall (Marlena Evans)
Outstanding Villain:	Jason Brooks (Peter Blake)
Outstanding Female Scene Stealer:	Louise Sorel (Vivian Alamain)
Hottest Soap Couple:	Robert Kelker-Kelly and Lisa Rinna (Bo and Billie)

Twelfth Annual Awards Presentation (1996)

Favorite Show:	*Days of our Lives*
Hottest Male Star:	Peter Reckell (Bo Brady)
Outstanding Supporting Actress:	Louise Sorel (Vivian Alamain)
Outstanding Villainess:	Alison Sweeney (Samantha Brady)

Thirteenth Annual Awards Presentation (1997)

Outstanding Villain:	Joseph Mascolo (Stefano DiMera)
Outstanding Female Showstopper:	Louise Sorel (Vivian Alamain)
Hottest Romance:	Austin Peck and Christie Clark (Austin and Carrie)

Weddings

English groom's cake

This groom's cake is considerably streamlined from the traditional version, which takes longer to bake and age (a year) than many modern marriages last.

2 cups raisins or currants
2 cups chopped candied fruit, such as pineapple
      and citron
1 cup candied cherries, chopped
½ cup cognac, brandy or bourbon (optional)
2 cups water
2 tablespoons vegetable oil
2 eggs
2 cups walnut pieces
2 packages date or nut bread mix
1 cup corn syrup (optional)

● Toss together the raisins, candied fruit, cherries, and cognac. Stir and allow to marinate several hours or overnight. This step may be omitted.

● Preheat the oven to 350°. Grease and flour the bottom and sides of a 12-cup fluted tube pan or a 10-inch tube pan.

● In a large bowl, combine the water, oil, and eggs. Add the raisins, candied fruit, cherries, walnuts, and bread mix. Stir by hand until well-combined.

● Pour into the prepared pan. Bake for 1 hour and 15 to 25 minutes or until a tester inserted in the center comes out clean.

● Cool the cake in the pan for 30 minutes. Loosen the edges and remove from the pan. Cool completely. Wrap tightly and refrigerate overnight.

● *To glaze the cake before serving:* Warm the corn syrup. It should be warm, not hot. If desired, decorate the cake with pieces of the candied fruit and whole nuts. Brush on the warm corn syrup. Store in refrigerator for up to 2 weeks or freeze for up to 3 months. Slice thinly to serve.

MAKES 24 TO 36 SERVINGS.

Raspberry (or apricot) filled butter cookies

Light and buttery, these cookies will go fast. Make two batches if you've got the time and patience.

$^1/_2$	cup sugar
3	cups flour
$1^1/_2$	sticks butter
$1^1/_2$	sticks unsalted (sweet) butter
1	teaspoon vanilla extract
1	tablespoon lemon juice
1	(8-ounce) jar raspberry (or apricot) preserves
$^1/_4$	cup confectioners' sugar

- Sift together the sugar and flour into a large bowl. Cut the butter into 1-inch-thick pieces. Using a pastry blender or two knives, blend the butter into the flour mixture until crumbly and the texture of rice.

- Add the vanilla and use a wooden spoon to work the mixture into a smooth dough. Cover the bowl with plastic wrap and refrigerate. Chill completely, at least 1 hour.

- Remove the dough from the refrigerator and cut into 3 pieces of equal size. Roll out each piece $^1/_8$-inch thick between 2 sheets of floured waxed paper. Lift the top sheets occasionally during rolling to prevent sticking.

- When the dough is rolled to the desired thickness, transfer the dough on waxed paper to a baking sheet and place in the freezer. This step makes handling this delicate dough much easier. If the dough softens too much, return it to freezer so it can firm up.

- Preheat the oven to 325°.

- Meanwhile, add the lemon juice to the raspberry jam in a small saucepan. Place over low heat just until melted. Pour the mixture through a strainer or fine colander, using the back of a spoon to force it through, and allow to cool. Do not force through any seeds or pieces of fruit.

- Remove 1 sheet of the rolled pastry from the freezer. Turn upside down on a second sheet of floured waxed paper. Peel off the top sheet and cut out 2-inch rounds with a cookie or biscuit cutter. Using a spatula, transfer the rounds to an ungreased baking sheet.

- Using a small cutter no more than 1-inch in diameter (a bottle cap will work), cut out the centers from half of the rounds. Using a spatula, transfer these doughnut-shaped rings to an ungreased baking sheet. Scraps of dough may be re-rolled and frozen for shaping more cookies.

- Bake the rings and rounds for 12 to 15 minutes or until just barely colored. Remove from the oven and allow to cool slightly. Carefully remove from the baking sheet and cool completely on a rack.

- Spread the rounds with raspberry jam, almost to the edges. If the jam is too congealed, reheat just so it spreads smoothly and evenly.

- Lay the rings on the rounds so the raspberry jam peeps through the holes. Sift a small amount of confectioners' sugar over each cookie.

MAKES ABOUT 4 DOZEN COOKIES.

Weddings

Gingered citrus punch

1¹/₂ *quarts lemon juice*
1¹/₂ *quarts orange juice*
6 *quarts bottled water*
8 *cups sugar*
1 *quart pineapple juice*
2 *quarts ginger ale (may substitute sparkling wine)*
1 *gallon lemon sherbet (optional)*
Frozen strawberries (optional)

- In a large wide-mouth container, combine the lemon juice, orange juice, water, sugar, and pineapple juice. Stir to dissolve the sugar.

- Refrigerate for several hours or place in a cooler, surrounded by ice.

- When ready to serve, add the chilled ginger ale.

- If desired, place scoops of lemon sherbet in the punch bowl and pour punch into the bowl.

- Or, garnish with slices of fresh fruit or frozen strawberries.

- *To freeze strawberries:* Place the strawberries in the compartments of an ice cube tray. Pour the ginger ale into the tray and freeze. Use as garnish in the punch.

MAKES 50 SERVINGS.

Hope's Love Letter to Bo

Only two people knew the combination to Tom Horton's puzzle box: Tom and Hope. So, when Gina was trying to prove her identity, Alice Horton gave her the box, figuring that if Gina could open it, she would be one step closer to proving she was Hope. No one knew that within the box was the following letter, and as Bo read it, Gina spoke the words aloud, proving conclusively to everyone present her true identity.

Dear Bo:

I'm writing this letter to you on the morning of our wedding. I'm going to put it in a special place, and one day, years from now, I'll show it to you.

Gran gave me the idea. She wrote a letter to Grandpa on their wedding day. She wrote all her feelings, her hopes, and dreams so that one day they could look back and remember how their life together began. I want us to do that, too. As I write, I'm looking into the future, to that day when you'll finally read this. What will we be like? How will we feel when that day finally arrives?

I'll be leaving for the church in a little while. I'll take your hand and pledge my love to you for all eternity. I am so excited, so happy. And yes, even a little frightened, too. But mostly I am filled with this incredible emotion that wells up inside me. It overflows and reaches every part of me, giving me such joy, such happiness. It's such a wonderful emotion . . . I'm not sure what to call it.

A little word like love doesn't seem big enough to describe it. But I guess there's no other word. So in the end, I'm back where I started . . . with no words to truly express the depth of my love, the scope of my joy, the certainty of my commitment.

I just want you to know that on this day, and every day hereafter, I will thank God for you. And I will show you that I love you, from the bottom of my heart and the depths of my soul. Forever.

Hope

SAMI AND AUSTIN'S PARIS WEDDING

A wedding should be a joyous occasion, but the day that Sami Brady and Austin Reed were married in Paris was an absolute nightmare. Carrie Brady was actually Austin's intended bride. Taking to heart Celeste Perrault's prophecy that she must marry Austin as rapidly as possible or live to regret it, Carrie planned her wedding quickly while waiting for their French marriage license to become valid. It was to be a small affair attended by John Black, Marlena Evans, Kristen Blake, Billie Reed, Abe and Lexie Carver, and Mickey Horton. The hotel suite was beautifully decorated, and Carrie had acquired an exquisite antique-looking lace dress. She even remembered to hire a cameraman to videotape the happy event. But Carrie stepped aside and allowed Austin to "marry" Sami in a sham ceremony so that Sami's baby Will, whom Austin believed to be his son and who had been kidnapped and brought to Paris, could be readmitted to the United States. Despite Austin's repeated reminders that it was a wedding in name only, Sami considered it to be real. She was even mean-spirited enough to purchase an exact copy of Carrie's dress to wear and insisted on carrying Carrie's bouquet. Afterward, Sami coerced everyone into attending the reception Carrie had planned at a nearby restaurant to make the bogus nuptials appear authentic on video. This was a wedding that no one in attendance will soon forget.

M E N U

CREAMED MUSHROOMS ON TOAST TRIANGLES

SCRAMBLED EGGS AND HAM WITH TOMATOES
AND ANCHOVIES

LOBSTER (OR SHRIMP) WITH HERBED RICE

PEACH (OR APPLE) BREAD PUDDING WITH CARAMEL SYRUP

Creamed mushrooms on toast triangles

1	*pound firm fresh white mushrooms, rinsed, dried, and sliced (trim and chop stems, if desired)*
1½	*cups heavy cream*
1½	*teaspoons salt or to taste*
1	*teaspoon pepper or to taste*
½	*teaspoon ground nutmeg or to taste*
4	*pieces of firm white bread, toasted, crusts removed*

- Place the sliced fresh mushrooms caps (and chopped stems) in a large skillet over medium heat. Toss or stir gently for 3 to 4 minutes until the mushrooms begin to give up their liquid. Stir in the cream, salt, pepper, and nutmeg. Lower heat to simmer.

- Cook, stirring occasionally, until the mushrooms are tender and the cream thickens, 10 to 15 minutes. Adjust seasoning to taste.

- Trim the crusts to form neat toast squares. Cut the squares diagonally at the corners to create 4 triangles. Arrange 2 triangles on each place, sides touching , points out. Spoon the creamed mushrooms over the toast. Serve warm.

MAKES 8 SERVINGS.

Scrambled eggs and ham with tomatoes and anchovies

4	large, firm, ripe tomatoes or 1 (16-ounce) can tomatoes
1	teaspoon herbes de Provence (an herb blend) or 1 teaspoon dried leaf thyme
2	anchovy fillets (optional)
2	teaspoons pepper or to taste, divided
2	teaspoons salt or to taste, divided
2	tablespoons butter
2	tablespoons olive oil
¹/₂	cup finely chopped shallots or onion
1	cup coarsely chopped, thinly sliced ham or Canadian bacon
10	eggs, divided

- If using fresh tomatoes, cut off the tops. Holding cut-side down, squeeze the tomato seeds into a strainer positioned over a bowl to catch the juices. Use your fingers to scrape out the seeds. Discard the seeds. Using a spoon, scoop out the pulp and chop finely. Discard the shells of tomato peel. Combine the juice with the chopped pulp in a small saucepan.

- If using canned tomatoes, drain the can juices. Chop the tomatoes, reserving the juice released during chopping, and place in a small saucepan. Pick out the seeds, if desired.

- Add the herbes de Provence or thyme to the tomatoes and cook, stirring frequently, over low heat until the tomatoes are soft and the juice evaporates and thickens, about 10 minutes. Stir in the anchovy fillets, mashing with the back of a spoon to combine evenly with the tomatoes. Add ¹/₂ teaspoon pepper or to taste. Adjust seasoning with a dash of salt, if desired. Remove from heat and reserve.

- Heat the butter and olive oil in a large skillet over low heat, just until bubbly. Add the shallots and ham or Canadian bacon and cook until the shallots are soft, about 3 minutes. Do not allow the shallots to brown. Remove from heat and reserve.

- Crack 9 eggs into a mixing bowl, beating with a fork or a whisk until frothy and uniform in color. Beat in the remaining salt and pepper, or to taste. Break the remaining egg into another small bowl. Beat lightly and reserve.

- Return the skillet to heat and add the large bowl of beaten eggs to the pan. Cook over low heat, stirring gently with a spatula, until the eggs are set but still soft. Remove from heat and fold in the remaining egg to stop the cooking. Stir in the tomato mixture and adjust seasoning to taste. Serve warm.

MAKES 8 SERVINGS.

Weddings

Lobster (or shrimp) with herbed rice

3	tablespoons Dijon mustard
1	tablespoon white wine or champagne vinegar
2	tablespoons water
$^{1}/_{2}$	cup extra-virgin olive oil
$^{1}/_{2}$	cup canola oil
2	tablespoons cold milk
1	teaspoon capers, well-drained
1	teaspoon dried tarragon
$^{1}/_{2}$	cup fresh parsley leaves, loosely packed
$^{1}/_{2}$	teaspoon salt or to taste
$^{1}/_{2}$	teaspoon pepper or to taste
2	cups long grain white rice
1	(8-ounce) package green peas
$^{1}/_{4}$	cup heavy cream, well-chilled
1	pound cooked lobster meat, cut into bite-size pieces, or 1 pound cooked medium shrimp (use a combination, if desired)*

2 to 3 avocados, peeled, seeded, and sliced, for garnish
Lemon wedges or thin slices of lemon for garnish

- Combine the mustard, vinegar, and water in the work bowl of a food processor or a blender container. With the motor running, add the olive oil, canola oil, and milk in a thin stream.

- When all is combined and the mixture begins to look like mayonnaise, stop the motor and scrape down the sides. Add the capers, tarragon, parsley, salt, and pepper. Process again, about 10 seconds longer, until the capers and herbs are finely chopped and evenly distributed throughout the sauce.

- The sauce may be stored for up to 1 week in the refrigerator. Thin with water or lemon juice, if needed.

- Cook the rice according to package directions, toss to separate grains, and allow to cool. Cook the peas according to the package directions and allow to cool. Toss together the rice and peas.

- To prepare for serving, beat the heavy cream until stiff peaks form. Fold the whipped cream into the green mayonnaise. Set aside about ¹/₂ cup green mayonnaise. Blend the remaining green mayonnaise into the rice, mixing well to coat each grain evenly. Toss the seafood with the reserved mayonnaise, mixing well to coat the seafood lightly but evenly.

- To serve, place a dollop of rice on each plate and top with several pieces of lobster or shrimp. Garnish with avocado slices, a lemon wedge, or a slice of lemon.

MAKES 8 SERVINGS.

- *Shortcut:* Combine 1¹/₄ cups prepared mayonnaise, 3 tablespoons Dijon mustard, and 1 tablespoon white wine or champagne vinegar. Place 1 teaspoon well-drained capers, 1 teaspoon dried leaf tarragon, and ¹/₂ cup fresh parsley leaves in a blender or food processor. Process until finely chopped. Scrape finely chopped herbs into the green mayonnaise and blend well. Adjust seasoning to taste with pepper and salt. Add 1 to 2 teaspoons lemon juice, if desired.

*Most fish markets and supermarket fish counters sell cooked shrimp and lobster. Or they will cook it for you. Make sure you order cooked weight.

SAMANTHA BRADY REED

Although Sami's life began uneventfully enough, it turned traumatic when her "father" (Roman II, a.k.a. John Black) came home with a new face, and it became even more trying when it appeared her mother, Marlena Evans, had been killed. It was a joyous day for Sami when her real father (Roman) and mother were reunited. But when she caught Marlena and John, who still had passionate feelings for each other, making love on the conference table at Titan Industries, Sami's life went into a downward spiral. She became bulimic, then altered hospital records and kidnapped her baby sister, Belle. After being raped and later humiliated at the perpetrator's trial, Sami turned her anger toward stepsister Carrie and vowed to take revenge by stealing Carrie's boyfriend, Austin Reed. She became pregnant, drugged Austin and tricked him into sleeping with her, and later stopped Carrie's wedding to Austin and skillfully used baby Will to manipulate Austin. When Will was kidnapped and taken to Paris, Sami turned that to her advantage and got Austin to marry her in a bogus ceremony so the baby could be readmitted to the United States. Kate Roberts eventually exposed Sami as a manipulative monster, which pushed Sami to spoil her sister's happiness once again—by continuing to feign amnesia after recovering her memory to make Austin feel sorry for her. That ploy worked for a while, but Carrie, Mike Horton, and Sami's fraternal twin, Eric, uncovered her scheme. Carrie and Austin finally married, and while Sami may be out, she is definitely not down for the count.

Peach (or apple) bread pudding with caramel syrup

Use seasonal fruit for this dessert. When fresh peaches are available in the summer, choose them. Apples are delicious in the fall and winter.

2 *pounds peaches or apples, peeled and thinly sliced to make 3 cups*
$^1/_2$ *stick unsalted butter*
4 *cups stale French bread, broken into bite-size pieces*
2 *cups milk*
4 *eggs, lightly beaten*
1 *cup sugar*
1 *tablespoon vanilla extract*

- Preheat the oven to 350°. Lightly coat a 13x9-inch baking dish with butter or vegetable cooking spray.

- Place the peaches or apples in a medium saucepan along with the butter. Cook over medium heat until the fruit is soft, about 5 minutes. Remove from heat and allow to cool slightly.

- In a large mixing bowl, combine the bread and milk. Stir together the eggs and sugar. Add to the bread mixture, stirring well. Let sit for 10 minutes. Stir in the cooked fruit and the vanilla. Turn the mixture into the prepared baking dish.

- Place the baking dish in a larger dish and pour in enough hot water to come 1 inch up the sides of the bread-pudding dish.

- Place in the oven and bake for 45 minutes to 1 hour or until center is set and a knife inserted in the center comes out almost clean. The top should be light brown. Remove from the oven and allow to cool. Cut into 3x4-inch squares. Serve warm or at room temperature, drizzled with Caramel Syrup (recipe follows).

MAKES 10 TO 12 SERVINGS.

Caramel syrup

1 *cup sugar*
1 *cup boiling water*

- Place the sugar in a small, heavy-bottomed saucepan over low heat. Cook, without stirring, until the sugar melts and turns golden.

- When the sugar is completely melted, stir in the boiling water and cook for 3 to 4 minutes until the syrup is a dark golden color. Allow to cool. Store in the refrigerator for up to 1 month.

- *Shortcut:* Use bottled caramel sauce.

BO AND BILLIE'S TRATTORIA WEDDING

Be careful what you wish for because you just might get it! Billie Reed was hoping that going to Rome and posing as Bo Brady's fiancé would change their relationship. After all, in what better place could hope spring eternal than the Eternal City itself? But Bo showed no sign of responding to the romance that surrounded the couple, and it was a shock to both Billie and Bo when JL King arranged to hold their wedding at a popular trattoria. Billie was frantically searching for a dress when a stylist friend offered to loan her a dress being worn by a Titan model. Billie accepted, never suspecting that the model was Hope Brady. To further complicate matters, King sent wedding invitations to Hope and Franco Kelly and arranged for Hope to serve as maid of honor. Needless to say, it was a difficult ceremony for all involved, and while the principals may not have enjoyed the sumptuous Italian feast, the guests found it to be a culinary treat. Yes, Billie got her wish when she married the man of her dreams—but in her heart she knew that she was not Bo's first choice.

MENU

BOW-TIE PASTA WITH ARTICHOKES

FIRE-ROASTED CHICKENS

EGGPLANT WITH YELLOW PEPPER

TIRAMISU

Bow-tie pasta with artichokes

2   tablespoons butter or extra-virgin olive oil
      (or a combination)
1/4   cup chopped onion
2   ounces prosciutto or cooked ham, finely chopped
1/2   cup canned Italian tomatoes and their liquid or
      chopped fresh tomato and juice
1   (8-ounce) package frozen artichoke hearts, thawed
      and finely chopped
1   tablespoon dried basil leaves, crushed
1/4   teaspoon salt or to taste
1/4   teaspoon pepper or to taste
1/2   pound bow-tie or other pasta, cooked according to
      package directions and drained
2 to 4 tablespoons grated Parmesan cheese, divided

- Place the butter or olive oil in a medium skillet over medium heat. Heat to melt. Add the onion and prosciutto. Cook, stirring, until onion is soft, about 3 to 5 minutes. Do not brown. Reduce heat if necessary.

- Stir in the tomatoes, breaking them into small pieces with the back of a spoon. Add the artichokes and basil.

- Cook over low heat, stirring frequently, until the artichokes are tender. Add salt and pepper to taste.

- Toss the pasta with the sauce and serve. Sprinkle each serving with 1 tablespoon Parmesan cheese.

**MAKES 2 MAIN COURSE SERVINGS
OR 4 FIRST COURSE SERVINGS.**

Fire–roasted chickens

1   (3-pound) roasting chicken or 4 Cornish game hens
4 to 5 tablespoons lemon juice
3 to 4 tablespoons extra-virgin olive oil
1 to 2 tablespoons whole black peppercorns,
        coarsely crushed
2 to 4 teaspoons salt, divided
1 to 2 tablespoons coarsely ground black pepper

- Using poultry shears, split the chicken or hens lengthwise along the backbone. Open the bird(s) flat and press down with the heel of your hand to flatten as much as possible. Tuck wings under. The bird(s) should be as flat as possible for even cooking. If you know a good butcher, ask him to do this for you.

- Place the chicken or hens in a resealable plastic bag and add the lemon juice, oil, and black peppercorns. Turn the bag several times to mix marinade ingredients and evenly coat the chicken. Set aside for 30 minutes. Refrigeration is not necessary for this short amount of time.

- Light the charcoal in a grill or preheat the oven broiler. If using charcoal, allow the flames to die out. Coals should be red but not flaming.

- Remove the chicken or hens from the marinade, allowing any excess to drip back into the bag. Season the chicken or hens with salt to taste. Reserve the marinade.

- Place the chicken or hens on the grill, skin-side down, or on a broiler pan, with the skin side toward the heat. Cook until the skin is evenly browned, about 10 to 15 minutes. Baste occasionally with the marinade. Turn and cook the other side, basting occasionally, until done, about 10 to 15 minutes or longer.

- To test for doneness, pierce the thick part of the thigh with a fork or tip of a knife. The chicken or hens are done when the juices run clear.

- Remove the bird(s) from the grill or broiler and season to taste with salt and coarsely ground black pepper.

- To serve the whole chicken, cut it into quarters (2 half-breasts with wings and 2 thigh-legs). Serve hens whole or split lengthwise into halves.

MAKES 4 SERVINGS.

BILLIE REED

Billie Reed came to Salem to start a new life, but she had trouble overcoming her old one. When Billie lost her job as a result of cocaine abuse, brother Austin's girlfriend Carrie Brady offered to share her apartment and Carrie's uncle Bo got Billie a job at Casey's Roadhouse. But the road to redemption was surrounded by thorns, and if not for Bo, Billie wouldn't have made it out of the thicket. Deserted by her mother and turned onto drugs and sexually abused by her father, Curtis, Billie had a textbook case of low self-esteem. A series of misadventures caused by Curtis's return brought Billie into closer proximity to Bo. And while it wasn't love at first sight for Bo, Billie was destined to be the woman to replace wife Hope in Bo's heart. Billie won a fledgling cosmetic company in a pool game, but just as the enterprise began to enjoy a modicum of success, Kate Roberts maneuvered the company away from Billie, who turned out to be Kate's daughter. Life continued to be difficult for Billie—she was tried for her father's murder and exonerated, and her first wedding to man-of-her-dreams Bo was halted when it was revealed that amnesia victim Gina might really be Hope, who had been presumed dead. After Gina signed papers declaring Hope legally dead, Billie at long last married Bo, but Gina later regained her memory, recalling that she was in fact Hope. Billie left for Europe so that Bo could sort out his feelings, but when she returned to Salem she discovered that Bo and Hope were again in love. Billie has always been true to herself and now must decide if she can settle for being Bo's second choice.

Weddings

Eggplant with yellow pepper

1	(1 ¹/₂ to 2-pound) eggplant, unpeeled
1	large yellow bell pepper, seeded and ribs removed
¹/₂	cup extra-virgin olive oil, plus additional, as needed
¹/₂	cup chopped onion
2	cloves garlic, crushed
1	teaspoon salt or to taste
¹/₂	teaspoon black pepper or to taste
¹/₄	cup chopped fresh basil

- Cut the eggplant into ¹/₂-inch cubes. Cut the bell pepper into pieces about the same size and set aside.

- Heat the olive oil in a medium skillet over medium heat. Add the onion and cook until soft, about 3 to 5 minutes. Do not brown.

Reduce heat if necessary. Add the garlic and bell pepper. Cook for 3 to 5 minutes, until the garlic and pepper begin to soften.

- Stir in the eggplant and lower heat. Cook, stirring frequently to prevent the eggplant from sticking, until it is light brown at the edges and tender but still firm, not mushy. Season to taste with salt and black pepper. Transfer the eggplant to a medium bowl and allow to cool to room temperature.

- If the eggplant appears dry, sprinkle with additional olive oil and garnish with a sprinkling of basil before serving. Serve at room temperature.

MAKES 4 SERVINGS.

Tiramisu

The name literally means "pick me up," a direct reference to the jolt your taste buds will receive when they're hit with the brandy and coffee-flavored mascarpone (Italian cream cheese) layered between ladyfingers or slices of pound cake. Popularized by the movie Sleepless in Seattle, *this Italian dessert has become an international favorite.*

3	*tablespoons very strong coffee, preferably espresso*
2	*tablespoons brandy, divided*
3	*large eggs, separated*
¹/₂	*cup sugar*
8	*ounces mascarpone or cream cheese, softened to room temperature*
1	*teaspoon vanilla extract*
24	*ladyfingers or 12 slices of pound cake, sliced ¹/₄-inch thick*
2	*tablespoons cocoa, divided*
1	*teaspoon nutmeg*

Raspberries, blueberries, or strawberries for garnish

- Combine the coffee and 1 tablespoon brandy in a small bowl; reserve.

- Place the egg whites in a medium bowl and beat with electric beaters on high speed until stiff and glossy but not dry; reserve.

- In a clean bowl, combine the egg yolks and sugar. Using electric beaters, beat until thick and lemon-colored, about 2 minutes. Beat in 1 tablespoon brandy. Add the mascarpone and vanilla and blend well with electric beaters. Using a large spatula, fold the egg whites into the mascarpone mixture.

- Place a single layer of 12 ladyfingers in an 8-inch square baking dish. If using pound cake, cut each slice into pieces and arrange to make a single layer in the baking dish.

- Using a pastry brush, soak the ladyfingers or pound cake with half the coffee-brandy mixture.

- Spread about half the mascarpone mixture over the ladyfingers or pound cake. Sift 1 tablespoon cocoa over the top.

- Repeat layers with the remaining ladyfingers or pound cake, coffee-brandy mixture, and mascarpone. Cover and refrigerate at least 3 hours or overnight.

- To serve, sprinkle the top with the remaining cocoa and nutmeg. Spoon into shallow bowls or onto dessert plates. Garnish with fresh berries, if desired.

MAKES 8 SERVINGS.

Note: The eggs in this recipe are uncooked. Avoid this recipe if you are concerned about eating raw eggs.

CARRIE AND AUSTIN'S SALEM WEDDING

Turnabout is definitely fair play, and in 1997 Carrie Brady turned the tables on sister Sami by taking Austin Reed as her groom and commandeering the wedding Sami had arranged. Sami had finally managed to convince Austin that Carrie and Mike Horton were in Los Angeles as lovers. In despair, and believing that he was the father of Sami's son Will, Austin proposed to Sami. No one could dissuade him, not even Carrie, who had returned to Salem to try to stop the wedding. As the wedding began, Roman fainted as he escorted Sami down the aisle—a ploy to give Eric Brady more time to uncover the scheming Sami's real agenda. Eric and Carrie raced to University Hospital and, with Mike's help, found test results that proved Austin was not Will's father and that Sami had been lying all along. Carrie rushed to the church and stopped the wedding in the nick of time. Nearly everyone was shocked to learn that Sami had duped them into believing she still had amnesia and that Austin was not Will's father. Carrie and Austin, whose attempts to marry had been thwarted for two years, ignored the advice of friends and family and rushed to the altar to enter into a union they both thought they wanted. Only time will tell if their previous separation and Carrie's friendship with Mike have damaged their relationship sufficiently to prevent the couple from finding true happiness.

M E N U

SEAFOOD APPETIZER OF OYSTERS
AND CLAMS ON THE HALF SHELL, BOILED SHRIMP,
AND CRAB CLAWS WITH A TRIO OF SAUCES:
MIGNONETTE, REMOULADE, AND COCKTAIL

SALAD OF FIELD GREENS AND WALNUTS
WITH BLUE CHEESE VINAIGRETTE

ROAST VEAL CHOPS
WITH PEARL ONIONS AND PORT

MASCARPONE NOODLES WITH
STEAMED BROCCOLI FLORETS

HONEYMOON CAPPUCCINO

WEDDING CARROT CAKE
WITH CREAM CHEESE FROSTING

GROOM'S CHOCOLATE CHEESECAKE

Seafood appetizer

Serve impeccably fresh seafood on large, chilled plates. Make sure the fish market washes the oyster and clam shells well.

16 *(each) oysters and clams on the half shell*
32 *jumbo boiled shrimp*
16 *large crab claws, cooked and cracked*
Mignonette Sauce (recipe follows)
Remoulade Sauce (recipe follows)
Cocktail Sauce (recipe follows)

- Arrange the seafood on 8 well-chilled plates, allowing 2 (each) oysters and clams, 4 shrimp, and 2 crab claws per person.

- Serve with 3 sauces (recipes follow).

MAKES 8 SERVINGS.

Mignonette sauce

Juice from 1 lemon
1 cup champagne vinegar
1/4 cup finely chopped shallots
1 teaspoon salt or to taste
1 teaspoon pepper or to taste

● In a small bowl, combine the lemon juice, champagne vinegar, shallots, and salt and pepper to taste. Stir well. Serve in small ramekins for dipping or place about 1 teaspoon of the sauce on each oyster or clam on the half shell. Stir well each time to make sure that servings include ample portions of the shallots and seasonings, which will tend to settle to the bottom of the mixing bowl.

MAKES ABOUT 1 CUP.

Remoulade sauce

1 1/2 cups mayonnaise
3 teaspoons Dijon mustard
1 teaspoon anchovy paste (optional)
1 tablespoon finely chopped parsley
1 tablespoon drained, chopped capers
1 teaspoon dried chervil
1 to 2 teaspoons lemon juice or to taste

● In a small bowl, combine the mayonnaise, mustard, anchovy paste, parsley, capers, chervil, and lemon juice to taste. Blend well and refrigerate for at least 1 hour. Serve in small ramekins for individual service.

MAKES ABOUT 1 1/2 CUPS.

Cocktail sauce

1 cup ketchup
1 cup chili sauce
2 to 3 teaspoons prepared horseradish or to taste
1 to 2 tablespoons lemon juice or to taste
1 to 2 teaspoons Worcestershire sauce or to taste
2 to 3 drops red pepper sauce or to taste

● In a small bowl, combine the ketchup, chili sauce, horseradish, lemon juice, Worcestershire sauce, and red pepper sauce. Blend well. Refrigerate for 1 hour before serving. Serve in small ramekins for individual service.

MAKES 2 1/4 CUPS.

Salad of field greens and walnuts with blue cheese vinaigrette

American-made Maytag blue is the cheese of choice for this particular dressing. Note that the classic combination of blue cheese (in the salad) and port (with the veal) is recreated in the courses of this meal.

8 cups (2 quarts) mixed greens
1 cup walnuts, broken into pieces
Blue Cheese Vinaigrette (recipe follows)

● Rinse the greens and dry well. Place in a salad bowl or on individual plates. Drizzle Blue Cheese Vinaigrette over the greens and top with a sprinkling of walnut pieces.

MAKES 8 SERVINGS.

Weddings

Blue cheese vinaigrette

¹/₂ cup lemon juice or white wine vinegar
1¹/₂ cups olive oil
2   cloves garlic, finely chopped
1   teaspoon salt or to taste
1   teaspoon freshly cracked pepper or to taste
6   tablespoons crumbled blue cheese
2   tablespoons finely chopped parsley

● Combine the lemon juice or vinegar, olive oil, garlic, and salt and pepper to taste in a small bowl or jar with tight-fitting lid. Stir well or shake vigorously to combine the ingredients. Add the blue cheese and parsley, and stir or shake lightly to combine. Chill for 1 hour before serving.

MAKES ABOUT 2 CUPS.

Roast veal chops with pearl onions and port

8   (6- to 7-ounce) veal chops, at least 1-inch thick
2   teaspoons salt or to taste, divided
2   teaspoons freshly cracked pepper or to taste, divided
1   tablespoon olive oil
3   cups pearl onions, no bigger than large marbles
¹/₂ cup chopped fresh sage (optional)
1   cup port wine
¹/₂ cup chicken stock
2 to 4 tablespoons butter

● Rinse and dry the veal chops. Season to taste on both sides with salt and pepper.

● Heat a large, heavy-bottomed skillet over medium-high heat. Add the olive oil. Cook the veal chops, 4 at a time, until brown on both sides and medium-rare to medium inside, about 3 to 5 minutes per side.

● Remove the veal chops from the pan and lightly cover with foil to keep warm.

● Add the pearl onions to the pan. Reduce heat to medium-low. Cook and stir the onions until well-browned, about 5 minutes. Add the chopped sage and cook briefly.

● Add the port and chicken stock; bring the liquid to a boil. Lower heat slightly and cook until the liquid is reduced by one-third, to make about 1 cup.

● Remove from heat. Swirl in the butter, 1 tablespoon at a time, to reach the desired thickness. Add salt and pepper to taste.

● Serve the veal chops with the pan sauce and pearl onions.

MAKES 8 SERVINGS.

AUSTIN REED

If ever a man has pulled himself up by his bootstraps, it's Austin Reed. Austin came to Salem with two talents: he could play the piano and he could box. For a while it appeared that he might have a career as a boxer, but when Austin's shady dealings caused his girlfriend Carrie Brady's face to be scarred by acid in revenge for his failure to throw a fight, Austin had to take a close look at his life. The force that drives Austin is his deep-seated need not to be like his father, Curtis, who abandoned his children Austin and Billie and beat his wife Kate. Austin has a big heart but doesn't realize just how terrific a person he really is. When Abby Deveraux needed a bone marrow transplant, Austin volunteered. When he had the opportunity to reunite with Carrie by working at Titan Industries, Austin gave up his fledgling television career to be with the woman he loved. And when he believed Carrie was in love with Mike Horton, Austin decided not to stand in their way. Austin proposed to Sami Brady and was willing to sacrifice his happiness to do the right thing for Sami and the son he thought was his. Austin couldn't believe that Sami had fooled him again, but Sami knew of Austin's insecurities and used them to manipulate him to her advantage—and totally ruined two and a half years of his life. But now that Austin is finally married to Carrie, he and Lucas Roberts have agreed they will both be Will's "father," which leaves malicious mom Sami out in the cold.

Mascarpone noodles with steamed broccoli florets

This is very similar to fettuccine Alfredo but even simpler. Using mascarpone (Italian cream cheese) makes a difference, although American cream cheese may be substituted.

16 ounces noodles, such as fettuccine
2 ounces mascarpone (Italian cream cheese), softened to room temperature
$^3/_4$ teaspoon salt or to taste
2 cups Steamed Broccoli Florets (recipe follows)
1 teaspoon freshly cracked pepper or to taste

- Bring a large potful of water to a boil. Stir in the noodles and cook according to package directions, about 10 minutes; drain.

- In a large bowl, beat the mascarpone with $^3/_4$ teaspoon salt with a wooden spoon to soften the cheese. If the cheese is too cold, beat in 1 to 2 tablespoons hot water or pasta cooking water.

- Remove half the mascarpone and reserve. Immediately after draining the pasta, transfer it to the bowl with the mascarpone. Toss the noodles with the mascarpone until the cheese is absorbed.

- Add the remaining mascarpone, Steamed Broccoli Florets, and pepper. Toss well again.

MAKES 8 SERVINGS.

Steamed broccoli florets

2 cups fresh broccoli florets
$^1/_2$ teaspoon nutmeg
$^1/_2$ cup water
$^1/_4$ teaspoon salt or to taste

- Rinse the broccoli. Combine the nutmeg, water, and salt in a saucepan or microwave-safe dish. Bring the water to a boil and add the broccoli, or place the broccoli over water in a steamer. Cover and cook until the broccoli is tender but still crisp, about 4 to 6 minutes.

- *To microwave:* Cover the dish and microwave on High for 4 to 6 minutes, stirring once halfway through cooking.

- Drain the broccoli well.

MAKES 4 SERVINGS.

Honeymoon cappuccino

3 cups strong fresh coffee or espresso
3 cups half & half
$^1/_2$ cup dark crème de cacao
$^1/_4$ cup rum
$^1/_4$ cup brandy
1 cup heavy cream, whipped (optional)
Ground nutmeg (optional)

- Combine the coffee, half & half, crème de cacao, rum, and brandy in a saucepan over medium heat. Do not allow to boil. Serve hot with a dollop of whipped cream lightly sprinkled with nutmeg, if desired.

MAKES 8 SERVINGS.

Wedding carrot cake with cream cheese frosting

1½ cups vegetable oil
1½ cups sugar
4 eggs, well-beaten
3 cups grated carrots
2 cups all-purpose flour
½ teaspoon salt
2 teaspoons baking soda
2 teaspoons cinnamon
2 teaspoons allspice
1 cup chopped pecans
1 cup golden raisins
1 teaspoon vanilla

- Preheat the oven to 325°. Grease and flour a 10x14-inch baking pan. (If using a 9x13-inch pan, you may have some batter left over. Discard or place in a small baking dish and bake just until set. The cook deserves a secret treat now and then.)

- Place the oil and sugar in a large bowl and mix until the sugar dissolves. Add the eggs and carrots; mix well.

- In another bowl, sift together the flour, salt, soda, cinnamon, and allspice. Add the dry ingredients to the carrot mixture in three parts, beating well after each addition.

- Stir in the pecans, raisins, and vanilla. Pour the batter into the prepared pan and bake for 55 to 60 minutes. The cake is done when a tester inserted in center comes out clean.

- Remove the cake to a rack and allow to cool for 20 minutes. Loosen the sides with a knife or spatula and carefully turn out of the pan. Allow the cake to cool completely before frosting.

MAKES 20 SERVINGS.

Cream cheese frosting

1 stick melted butter, cooled
1 (8-ounce) package cream cheese, softened to room temperature
2 cups confectioners' sugar, sifted before measuring
1 teaspoon vanilla extract

- Combine the cooled butter with the cream cheese and sugar in a medium bowl. Using electric beaters on high speed, beat until the mixture is light and fluffy.

- Spread on the top and sides of the cooled cake.

MAKES 1 CUP.

Groom's chocolate cheesecake

1 (9-ounce) package chocolate wafer cookies
1½ cups sugar, divided
½ cup melted butter, cooled
10 ounces bittersweet chocolate
4 (8-ounce) packages cream cheese, softened to room temperature
1 teaspoon vanilla extract
⅓ cup unsweetened cocoa
4 eggs
Whipped cream for garnish (optional)

- Break up the cookies and place in the work bowl of a food processor. Add ¼ cup sugar and process to form fine crumbs. Add the cooled butter and process until the crumbs stick together. Press the crumbs onto the bottom and up the sides of a 9x2½-inch springform pan.

- Preheat the oven to 350°.

- Place the chocolate in a heavy saucepan over very low heat. Stir constantly until melted and smooth. Remove from heat and reserve.

Weddings

- Place the cream cheese and 1¼ cups sugar in a large mixing bowl. Using electric beaters, beat on medium speed until well-blended and smooth. Beat in the cocoa. Add the eggs, one at a time, beating after each addition.

- Add the melted chocolate and vanilla. Beat just until smooth. Pour the filling into the crust.

- Bake until the center appears firm or set, about 50 minutes. Remove from the oven and place on a rack to cool. When the cake is cool, cover with aluminum foil and place in the refrigerator overnight.

- Remove the cake from the pan by running a knife around the pan sides to loosen the cake. Release the pan sides. Leave the cake on the base of the pan and transfer to a serving platter. Garnish with whipped cream, if desired.

MAKES 12 SERVINGS.

5 FAST AND FABULOUS

*L*osing your head? All tied up? Feel like you have only minutes to live? No one's life is as pressured as John Black's, but if you feel yours is running a close second, this is the chapter for you. For those nights when the cook is off (right!), you've forgotten to defrost, and take-out just won't do, why not try one of the following recipes? They're divided into four sections: dishes that require no cooking, those that require some quick basic cooking, dishes that go together quickly but require a bit of cooking time, and fast and simple after-school snacks. The time you save with these quick and easy dishes you can spend watching Days of our Lives.

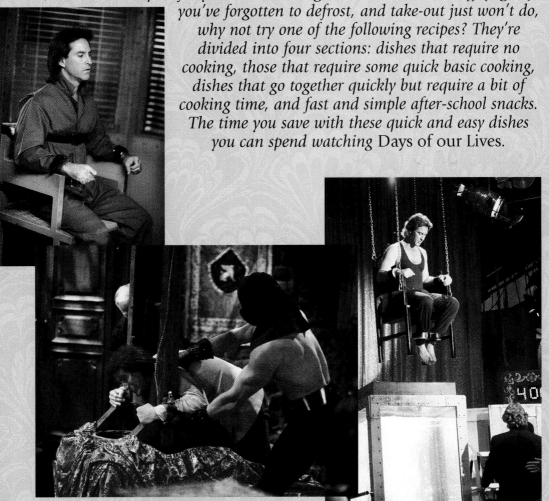

Fast and Fabulous

These dishes assemble without cooking.

*UNCLE CHIN'S CHICKEN SALAD WITH ASIAN MARINADE

KATE'S GREEK SALAD

*FRESH FRUIT WITH CREAMY VANILLA ALMOND SAUCE

These dishes require some quick basic cooking.

BROCCOLI AND OYSTER MUSHROOMS
WITH CHINESE SWEET AND SOUR SAUCE

CANADIAN BACON PIZZA WITH VIDALIA ONION MARMALADE

HOMEMADE GOURMET BURGER

*GRILLED TUNA STEAKS

*THIN SPAGHETTI WITH GARLIC, MUSHROOMS, AND PINE NUTS

STRAWBERRY PIE WITH ROMANOFF CREAM

* dishes lower in fat and calories.

These dishes go together quickly but require some cooking time. In about an hour or less, these dishes are done. Many of these are good for cooking in advance, as well.

BAKED SPAGHETTI

CRANBERRY CORNISH GAME HENS

*TEX-MEX MEATLOAF WITH PICANTE GRAVY

*ITALIAN SAUSAGE AND POTATOES
WITH PEPPERS AND ONIONS

CROCKPOT CHICKEN AND "HOMEMADE" NOODLES

*HONEY-PECAN CHICKEN BREASTS WITH *LEMON SAUCE

BAKED FRUIT CRISP

These are quick and easy after-school snacks.

EASY QUESADILLAS

PEANUT BUTTER AND COOKIE SANDWICHES

KATE ROBERTS

Okay, so she'll never win Mother of the Year, but it won't be for lack of trying. Maybe it's the guilt Kate feels for abandoning Austin and Billie when they were very young (husband Curtis Reed told her they were dead). Now that the family is reunited (after Kate finessed the Countess Wilhemina

cosmetics firm from Billie before she knew Billie was her daughter), Kate is going to extraordinary efforts to try to ensure their happiness. Kate just hopes younger son Lucas won't feel threatened by her efforts on behalf of Austin and Billie, and that he'll give up his dream girl Carrie. She also hopes Lucas will forgive her for not telling him Bill Horton is his real father. Kate moved to Salem to become president of Titan Publishing and Editor-in-Chief of Bella *magazine, where she met Victor Kiriakis and fell in love. It looked like smooth sailing until the journal she wrote more than 17 years before turned up, Vivian decided to re-stake her claim on Victor, and Sami dug up Kate's dirty laundy and started blackmailing her. What's a mother to do?*

Uncle Chin's chicken salad

1   cup cooked chicken breast meat, cut in bite-size pieces
Asian Marinade (recipe follows) or use a bottled
       marinade such as teriyaki and add 1 to 2
       tablespoons cider vinegar or rice wine vinegar
3   cups cooked spaghetti
2   tablespoons thinly sliced green onions, including
       green part
1 or 2 ribs celery, thinly sliced
3   cups shredded iceberg lettuce

- Place the chicken in a small bowl and add the Asian Marinade (or ³/₄ to 1 cup bottled sauce plus 2 to 3 tablespoons vinegar or to taste). Stir to coat the chicken evenly and set aside.

- Add the pasta, green onions, and celery to the chicken mixture and toss to combine and coat with dressing. Spoon the chicken and pasta mixture onto a bed of lettuce. Lightly drizzle any dressing that remains in the bowl over the lettuce.

MAKES 3 SERVINGS.

Asian marinade

2   tablespoons vegetable oil
1   tablespoon Asian sesame oil
2   tablespoons soy sauce
¹/₄   cup cider vinegar or rice wine vinegar
2   teaspoons grated fresh ginger
2   teaspoons sugar
¹/₂   teaspoon red pepper flakes
1   clove finely chopped garlic
1   tablespoon chopped fresh cilantro (optional)

- In a medium mixing bowl, combine the vegetable oil, sesame oil, soy sauce, vinegar, ginger, sugar, red pepper flakes, garlic, and cilantro, if using. Stir to blend.

MAKES 3 SERVINGS.

Kate's Greek salad

1   cucumber
1   teaspoon salt (divided) or to taste
2   large tomatoes, peeled
¹/₂   teaspoon sugar
1   (12-ounce) bag American (or your favorite) salad
       greens blend
¹/₂ to 1 cup thinly sliced rings of red onion or to taste
¹/₄   cup lemon juice or 2 tablespoons red wine vinegar
¹/₂   cup extra-virgin olive oil
2   teaspoons dried leaf oregano
3   ounces feta cheese (drained weight), crumbled
2   tablespoons capers, rinsed and drained (optional)
12   calamata (Greek black) olives

- Peel the cucumber and cut into thin slices. If the cucumber is large, cut in half lengthwise, then slice thinly.

- *Optional step:* Place the cucumber slices in a colander and sprinkle lightly with ¹/₂ teaspoon salt, tossing to coat evenly. Allow to drain for about 20 minutes.

- Meanwhile, cut the tomatoes into bite-size pieces and place in a large bowl. Sprinkle the tomatoes lightly with ¹/₂ teaspoon salt and sugar, tossing to coat evenly. Set aside about 10 minutes.

- Add the greens, onion, and drained cucumbers. Toss well to distribute ingredients evenly.

- Combine the lemon juice or vinegar, olive oil, and oregano in a jar with a tight-fitting lid. Shake well to combine. Pour over the salad and toss to distribute the ingredients and evenly coat with dressing.

- Scatter the crumbled feta, capers, and olives over the salad. Serve immediately.

MAKES 4 SERVINGS.

Fast and Fabulous

Fresh fruit with creamy vanilla almond sauce

1   (8-ounce) carton vanilla low-fat yogurt
1 to 2 drops almond extract or to taste
1   tablespoon chopped toasted almonds
2   cups fresh fruit, cut or sliced for eating with fingers or
         spearing with toothpicks (sliced apples, peaches or
         pears; whole or halved strawberries; bananas,
         cantaloupe, pineapple or watermelon cut in
         chunks; large raspberries or blackberries; cherries)
Lemon juice as needed

- Combine the yogurt, almond extract, and almonds. Cover and refrigerate for 1 hour.

- Prepare the fruit. Sprinkle fruit that may discolor with lemon juice; apples, peaches, and bananas are susceptible to discoloration. Toss the fruit to coat well.

- Serve the fruit with sauce for dipping or pour the sauce over the fruit in individual bowls.

MAKES 2 SERVINGS.

Broccoli and oyster mushrooms with Chinese sweet and sour sauce

1	pound fresh broccoli florets
1	(8-ounce) jar oyster mushrooms, drained, or 1 (4-ounce) can sliced water chestnuts, drained
2	green onions, sliced on the diagonal in 1-inch pieces
1	red bell pepper, seeded and membranes removed, cut in long, thin strips

● Place the broccoli in a microwave-safe container with lid, along with 1 tablespoon water. Microwave on High until tender, 4 to 6 minutes, stirring once during cooking. Drain and toss with the mushrooms or water chestnuts, onions, and red bell pepper strips. Keep warm. Pour warm Chinese Sweet and Sour Sauce (recipe follows) over the vegetables. Serve warm or at room temperature.

MAKES 4 TO 6 SERVINGS.

Chinese sweet and sour sauce

3	tablespoons soy sauce
2	teaspoons Oriental sesame oil
1	teaspoon honey
1/2	teaspoon grated fresh ginger or 1/4 teaspoon ground ginger
1/4	teaspoon dry mustard
1	teaspoon rice vinegar or cider vinegar

● Combine the soy sauce, sesame oil, honey, ginger, dry mustard, and vinegar in a microwave-safe glass 1-cup measure. Stir well. Microwave on High for 1 to 2 minutes, stirring occasionally, or until bubbly.

● Remove from the microwave and immediately pour over the hot vegetables. Serve warm or at room temperature. Also good with Grilled Tuna Steaks (see recipe on page 142).

MAKES ABOUT 1/2 CUP.

SHAWN-DOUGLAS BRADY

Shawn-Douglas is the heir apparent of Salem. He combines the best of both core families as Bo Brady is his father and Hope Williams (a Horton) is his mother. At only eleven years of age, he has sailed around the world, been deafened temporarily in an accident at Jencon Oil, been shot by drug dealers, and survived the "death" and return of his mother. When not playing baseball or soccer, Shawn-Douglas can be found at the Brady Pub with his grandparents, Shawn and Caroline, or at the Horton Center with great-grandmother Alice. Shawn-D's major goal in life is for his parents to reunite and restore his family.

Canadian bacon pizza with Vidalia onion marmalade

1   English muffin, split
2 to 3 tablespoons bottled pizza or spaghetti sauce
2 to 3 slices Canadian bacon, cut into pepperoni-size pieces
2   tablespoons Vidalia Onion Marmalade (recipe follows)
¹/₂   cup shredded mozzarella cheese

● Preheat the oven to 450°. Toast the English muffin. Spread the cut sides with pizza or spaghetti sauce. Top with the Canadian bacon pieces, onion marmalade, and shredded mozzarella. Place in the oven and bake just until the cheese melts, about 3 to 5 minutes.

MAKES 2 SMALL PIZZAS.

Movies in Which Days of our Lives *Has Appeared*

Close Encounters of the Third Kind **(1977)**

9 to 5 **(1980)**

Crocodile Dundee II **(1988)**

Mortal Thoughts **(1991)**

Single White Female **(1992)**

Son-In-Law **(1993)**

Heart And Soul **(1993)**

To Die For **(1995)**

The Cable Guy **(1996)**

Vidalia onion marmalade

1   large Vidalia or other sweet onion, sliced very thinly
2   tablespoons vegetable oil
2   tablespoons brown sugar
1   tablespoon cider vinegar

● In a skillet, combine the onion and vegetable oil over medium heat. When the onion begins to sizzle, lower heat. Do not allow the onion to brown. Cook very slowly, stirring frequently, until the onion is quite soft, 10 to 15 minutes.

● After about half the cooking time, add the brown sugar and cider vinegar. Stir and cook until the onion is soft and the liquid is thick and syrupy. Use as desired. Store in the refrigerator for up to 1 week.

MAKES 10 TO 12 (1-TABLESPOON) SERVINGS.

Homemade gourmet burger

¹/₂   pound ground sirloin patty
¹/₄   teaspoon seasoned salt, preferably a seasoning blend for steaks
¹/₄   teaspoon pepper
1   thick slice mozzarella cheese, about the same size as the meat patty
1   onion bun, split horizontally
2   teaspoons grainy mustard or to taste
2   teaspoons mayonnaise (optional)
4 to 5 leaves baby spinach
2 to 3 thin slices red onion

● Grill the sirloin patty over charcoal or on a gas grill. Cook until well-browned and grill-marked on one side. Turn and cook to the desired degree of doneness. Health authorities recommend medium, with little (if any) pink left in the middle. Burger aficionados insist on medium-rare, with a warm, pink center, just the safe side of bloody. The center should be warm, not cold.

- About 2 to 3 minutes before the patty is done, season each side with salt and pepper. Then top the sirloin patty with mozzarella cheese and cook until the cheese melts and oozes down the side.

- Meanwhile, separate the bun and spread the cut side of each half with mustard and mayonnaise, if desired. Layer shredded spinach on the bottom half of the bun. Place the burger on top of the spinach. Top with red onion.

- Serve with a kosher dill pickle and Homemade Potato Chips (see recipe on page 55).

MAKES 1 HAMBURGER.

CELESTE PERRAULT

It was obvious that Celeste was a woman of mystery when she first appeared during the Maison Blanche storyline, and for a while it seemed she was originally from New Orleans. Her psychic abilities and skill with tarot cards added to her mystique. As Stefano DiMera's loyal minion, she kept his secrets and, as it turned out, many of her own, as well. But a mother's love is the strongest, and Celeste's need to protect her daughter won out over her love for Stefano in the end. When Lexie's "Aunt Frankie" first appeared in Salem (and later in Aremid) and turned out to be Celeste—who was revealed as Lexie's birth mother—it wasn't too difficult to determine that Stefano was Lexie's biological father. Celeste kept the secret from him for years, but knowing the truth helps explain her resentment of Stefano's obsession with Marlena. Now, Celeste has spurned Stefano and is diligently discouraging Lexie from having any further contact with her father.

Fast and Fabulous

Grilled tuna steaks

4   (6-ounce) tuna steaks, about 1-inch thick
1/2 cup vegetable oil
1/4 cup lemon juice
2   tablespoon soy sauce
2   tablespoons finely chopped green onion
1   clove crushed garlic

● Rinse and dry the tuna steaks. Place in a resealable plastic bag. Combine the vegetable oil, lemon juice, soy sauce, green onion, and garlic. Stir together and pour over the tuna in the plastic bag. Squeeze out air and seal the bag. Turn the bag several times to coat the tuna well. Refrigerate while preparing the coals for grilling or preheating the oven broiler.

● When the coals are covered with gray ash, remove the steaks from the marinade, shaking off excess. Grill or broil for about 3 to 5 minutes per side. Serve warm or at room temperature.

MAKES 4 SERVINGS.

Thin spaghetti with garlic, mushrooms, and pine nuts

1   (8-ounce) package thin spaghetti
2   teaspoons vegetable oil or 1 teaspoon each oil
      and butter
2   cloves garlic, sliced very thinly
2   cups sliced fresh mushrooms
1/2 cup chopped onion
2   tablespoons all-purpose flour

Fast and Fabulous

1 cup milk
¹/₈ teaspoon nutmeg (optional)
¹/₂ cup frozen green peas, thawed
¹/₄ teaspoon salt or to taste
¹/₂ teaspoon freshly cracked black pepper or to taste
¹/₄ cup grated fresh Parmesan cheese
2 tablespoons Toasted Pine Nuts (see recipe on
      page 29)

- Place a large potful of water over high heat. When the water boils, stir in the spaghetti and cook according to package directions until tender but still firm, about 10 minutes. Drain and reserve. Toss lightly with oil to prevent sticking.

- Heat the oil (or oil and butter) in a large skillet over medium heat. Add the garlic and cook until brown around the edges. Add the mushrooms and chopped onion. Cook over low heat until the onion is softened and the mushrooms wilt, about 8 minutes.

- Add the flour, stirring constantly to coat ingredients well. Cook about 1 minute. Gradually add the milk, stirring constantly until thickened and bubbly. Add the nutmeg. Add the peas, stirring constantly for about 1 minute or until heated through. Adjust seasoning with salt and pepper.

- Combine the pasta, sauce, cheese, and pine nuts. Adjust seasoning with salt and pepper.

MAKES 4 SERVINGS.

LAURA SPENCER HORTON

Laura Horton is a psychiatrist at University Hospital, but she can really empathize with her patients since she was a "client" at Pine Haven for 18 years while in a catatonic state. It was there that she met Vivian Alamain and discovered they both abhorred Kate Roberts, whose affair with Laura's husband, Bill, had caused an unstable Laura's mental deterioration. Son Mike and daughter Jennifer were thrilled when Laura was released and returned to Salem. But they understood when mom, using a pseudonym, checked into the Meadows, a therapeutic retreat for individuals working on their interpersonal skills for romantic relationships. While there, Laura met "Clark," but it wasn't until after they had made love that each discovered who the other really was: Jen's mom and Jen's ex-husband, Jack Deveraux. When Laura returned home, Jen's nefarious fiancé, Peter Blake, thought Laura had overheard one of his schemes and gaslighted her, through the use of chemical fumes, into thinking she was losing her mind. After recovering, Laura discovered that Stefano and Peter were really alive. The evil pair kidnapped her, altered her memory with a laser, and drugged her so that she once again appeared on the verge of a mental collapse. But Laura's love for Jen and Jack proved stronger than the forces allied against her, and she rose to the occasion and helped Marlena reveal the treachery in Salem.

Fast and Fabulous

Strawberry pie with Romanoff cream

1   tablespoon strawberry gelatin mix (Jell-O)
1   cup hot water
3   tablespoons cornstarch
1   cup sugar
1   pint fresh strawberries, rinsed, dried, stems removed
        and sliced
1   (9-inch) prepared pie crust (see recipe on page 58)

● In a small saucepan over medium heat, combine the gelatin, hot water, cornstarch, and sugar. Cook and stir until thickened.

● Remove from heat and stir in the strawberries. Allow to cool.

● Pour into the baked pie crust and refrigerate. Serve with Romanoff Cream (recipe follows), if desired.

MAKES 8 SERVINGS.

Romanoff cream

1   (16-ounce) carton vanilla low-fat yogurt
½   cup firmly packed brown sugar
1 to 2 tablespoons sour cream (optional)

● Stir together the yogurt and brown sugar until the sugar is dissolved. Refrigerate until serving time. Spoon over fresh fruit or slices of Strawberry Pie (see preceding recipe).

● If a thicker cream is desired, and time allows, place the yogurt-brown sugar mixture in a colander lined with a double thickness of damp cheesecloth. Place the colander over a bowl and refrigerate several hours or overnight.

● Discard any liquid that has accumulated in the bowl. Yogurt cream should be thickened. If desired, stir in 1 to 2 tablespoons regular or reduced-fat sour cream. Serve with fruit, Strawberry Pie, or Fruit Crisp (see recipe on page 149).

MAKES 1½ TO 2 CUPS.

ABIGAIL JOHANNA DEVERAUX

Blonde and adorable, this daughter of Jack and Jennifer Horton Deveraux has a strong lease on life now. But it was touch and go when she was a baby and developed aplastic anemia, believed to have been caused by exposure to an illegal toxic dump site. Abby recovered after receiving a bone marrow transplant from Austin Reed, but when dad Jack found out that he was responsible for the dump site, he left town. Well, Jack's back and Abby is thrilled to have daddy in her life once again.

Baked spaghetti

12 ounces spaghetti
1   pound Italian sausage or lean ground beef
1   jar (about 32 ounces) spaghetti sauce
1   cup coarsely chopped green pepper or 1/2 cup roasted
        peppers, drained
1   cup black olives, sliced thick
1   (14-ounce) can artichoke hearts, drained and
        coarsely chopped (optional)
2   cups (8 ounces) grated mozzarella cheese
1/2 cup grated Parmesan cheese

● Bring a large potful of water to a boil. Stir in
  the spaghetti and cook until tender but still
  firm to the bite, about 10 minutes. Drain the
  spaghetti and set aside.

● Preheat the oven to 350˚. Crumble the Italian
  sausage or ground beef into a large skillet over
  medium heat. Cook until the meat is no longer
  pink. Add the fresh green (or roasted) pepper,
  black olives, and artichoke
  hearts. Stir and cook just
  until the vegetables wilt and
  are lightly browned at the
  edges. Pour off excess grease.

● Combine the drained spaghetti,
  Italian sausage or ground beef,
  and spaghetti sauce in a 9x13-
  inch baking dish.* Spread
  mozzarella cheese over all.
  Sprinkle with Parmesan cheese.

● Place in the oven for 30 minutes
  or until heated throughout and the
  cheese is melted.

MAKES 4 TO 6 SERVINGS.

*If desired, serve spaghetti sauce over pasta
and omit baking and the cheese topping.*

Cranberry Cornish game hens

1   (16-ounce) can whole-berry cranberry sauce
Juice of 1 lemon
2 to 4 Cornish game hens, split
Salt and pepper to taste

● Preheat the oven to 375˚. Combine the
  cranberry sauce and lemon juice. Place the
  Cornish game hens in a shallow baking dish.
  Season both sides with salt and pepper. Pour
  the cranberry sauce over the hens.

● Cover the dish with foil and bake for 30
  minutes. Remove the foil and bake until the
  hens are golden and juices run clear, about 20
  to 30 minutes longer.

MAKES 4 TO 8 SERVINGS.

145

Tex–Mex meatloaf with picante gravy

³/₄ *pound lean ground beef*
³/₄ *pound lean ground turkey*
³/₄ *cup bottled picante sauce (Pace's recommended), divided*
³/₄ *cup soft breadcrumbs*
2 *eggs, lightly beaten*
¹/₂ *teaspoon salt or to taste*
¹/₂ *teaspoon freshly cracked black pepper or to taste*

● Preheat the oven to 350°. Spray a 1¹/₂-quart ovenproof glass dish or large loaf pan with vegetable cooking spray.

● Crumble the beef and turkey into a large mixing bowl. Add ¹/₂ cup picante sauce, the breadcrumbs, eggs, salt, and pepper. Using your hands or a wooden spoon, mix well to combine all ingredients. Place in a loaf pan.

● Spread the remaining ¹/₄ cup picante sauce over the top. Bake for 1 to 1¹/₄ hours or until done throughout, with no pink remaining, and the sides pull away from the pan. Remove from the oven and let rest for 10 minutes before slicing. Serve with Picante Gravy (recipe follows).

MAKES 4 SERVINGS.

Picante gravy

1 *(1-ounce) envelope brown gravy mix with onions*
¹/₂ *cup bottled picante sauce (Pace's recommended)*
1¹/₂ *cups water*

● Place the gravy mix in a small saucepan. Stir in the picante sauce and water. Cook and stir over low heat until the mixture boils and thickens. Lower heat and simmer 1 minute. Remove from heat. Serve hot.

MAKES 4 SERVINGS.

ERIC BRADY

Sami's twin and the son of Roman and Marlena, Eric has spent the last several years living in Colorado with his maternal grandparents. His return to Salem was bad news for his sister as the two have a psychic bond that enables Eric to divine Sami's secrets. Eric bears the scars caused by Stefano DiMera's obsession with his parents: the loss of his father, being raised by a man (John Black) he thought was his father but wasn't, the subsequent loss of his mother for several years, and finally, the return of his real father, who had pretended to be dead. It's a sure bet that Eric has a number of secrets of his own, and if Sami is as good as Eric at divining hidden thoughts, he doesn't stand a chance of remaining an enigma.

Italian sausage and potatoes with peppers and onions

12 small new potatoes or 2 (16-ounce) cans new
        potatoes, drained
4   Italian-style lower-fat turkey sausages
1   tablespoon olive oil
3   cups onion, cut into large chunks
3   cups green peppers, seeded and cut into large chunks
1   teaspoon salt or to taste
1   teaspoon freshly cracked black pepper or to taste
1   teaspoon dried red pepper flakes to taste (optional)

● If using fresh potatoes, place the potatoes in a large saucepan with enough cold water to cover. Over high heat, bring the water to a boil. Reduce heat slightly to maintain a vigorous boil, and cook the potatoes until they can be easily pierced with a fork, about 20 minutes. Drain the potatoes and allow to cool. When cool enough to handle, cut the potatoes into quarters and set aside.

● If using canned potatoes, drain and set aside.

● Place the turkey sausages in a large skillet over medium-low heat. Cook gently so the sausage casings don't break. Cook until the sausages are golden and juices run clear, about 10 to 15 minutes. Remove from the skillet and reserve.

● If needed, add olive oil to the sausage-drippings skillet and place over medium-high heat. Add the potatoes and cook, stirring occasionally, until the edges are golden. Move the potatoes to the edge of the pan and add the onion. Cook, stirring occasionally, until the edges of the onion are golden.

● Add the green peppers and cook, stirring occasionally, until the peppers begin to soften. Add the salt, pepper, and red pepper flakes to taste, stirring well. Return the sausages to the pan and reduce heat to simmer. Cover and cook for about 5 minutes to allow flavors to develop.

MAKES 4 SERVINGS.

Crockpot chicken and "homemade" noodles

4   *chicken breast halves, with bone and skin*
2   *(14^1/$_2$-ounce) cans chicken stock*
1   *(8-ounce) carton frozen peas and carrots*
1   *(10^3/$_4$-ounce) can cream of chicken soup*
4 to 6 flour tortillas*
^{1}/$_2$ *teaspoon salt or to taste*
1   *teaspoon freshly cracked black pepper or to taste*
A few drops red pepper sauce or fresh lemon juice
     (optional)

- Place the chicken breast halves and chicken stock in a crockpot on High. Cook for 4 to 6 hours (8 hours on Low). Remove the chicken breasts from the stock and allow to cool. Remove the skin and bones; discard. Chop the chicken into bite-size pieces.

- Return the chicken to the crockpot. Stir in the peas and carrots and chicken soup. Cover and cook on High for 10 minutes. Trim the edges of the tortillas to form squares. Add the rounded-edge strips to the crockpot or discard, as desired.

- Stack the tortilla squares on a cutting board and cut into noodle-size strips. Add the strips to the crockpot and cook, uncovered, for 10 minutes. Cover and cook 10 minutes longer, until the strips are fluffy and tender.

- Season to taste with salt and pepper. Adjust seasoning with red pepper sauce or lemon juice just before serving.

MAKES 4 SERVINGS.

*If desired, substitute ^{1}/$_2$ pound wide noodles, cooked according to the package directions. Add to the crockpot along with the peas and carrots. Cook for 20 minutes. Season as above.

Honey–pecan chicken breasts with lemon sauce

^{1}/$_4$ *cup honey*
^{1}/$_4$ *cup Dijon mustard*
4   *boneless, skinless chicken breast halves*
1   *teaspoon salt or to taste*
^{1}/$_2$ *teaspoon freshly cracked black pepper or to taste*
^{1}/$_2$ *cup finely ground pecans*

- Preheat the oven to 350°. Spray a shallow baking dish with vegetable cooking spray. Combine the honey and mustard. Season the chicken breasts with salt and pepper. Spread the honey-mustard on both sides of the chicken. Place the chicken breasts in a prepared dish. Coat the top of each breast with ground pecans.

- Place in the oven and bake for 1 hour or until the chicken can be easily pierced with a fork. Serve with Lemon Sauce (recipe follows).

MAKES 4 SERVINGS.

Lemon sauce

1   *(14^1/$_2$-ounce) can chicken stock*
3   *tablespoons instant-blend flour*
^{1}/$_2$ *teaspoon salt or to taste*
^{1}/$_2$ *teaspoon freshly ground black pepper or to taste*
1 to 2 tablespoons lemon juice or to taste

- Place the chicken stock in a small saucepan over medium heat. Stirring constantly, gradually add the flour. Use a whisk or the back of a spoon to break up any lumps. Continue cooking and stirring until the mixture begins to boil.

- Lower heat to simmer. Add salt and black pepper to taste. Stir in lemon juice to taste. Simmer for 10 to 20 minutes. Serve with Honey-Pecan Chicken. Also good with baked chicken, fish, or pork chops.

MAKES 1¹/₂ CUPS.

Baked fruit crisp

¹/₂   *stick plus 1 tablespoon butter, softened to room temperature*
1   *cup firmly packed brown sugar*
³/₄   *cup all-purpose flour*
4   *cups sliced fruit, tart apples, pears or peaches (peeled), plums (unpeeled)*
1 to 2 tablespoons lemon juice

- Preheat the oven to 350°. Spray an 8x8-inch baking pan with vegetable cooking spray or lightly coat with butter.

- In a medium bowl, combine the butter, brown sugar, and flour until well-mixed and crumbly.

- Toss the fruit slices with the lemon juice, then place the fruit in the baking pan. Sprinkle the crumble mixture over the fruit. Bake for 1 hour. If desired, serve with Creamy Vanilla Almond Sauce (see recipe on page 138) or Romanoff Cream (see recipe on page 144).

MAKES 6 SERVINGS.

Fast and Fabulous

Easy quesadillas

2   *flour tortillas*
1/4 *cup shredded cheddar, mozzarella, or Monterey*
        jack cheese
1   *tablespoon salsa or to taste (optional)*

- Place 1 tortilla on a paper towel. Spread cheese almost to the edges of the tortilla. Sprinkle salsa over the cheese, if desired. Top with the second tortilla. Holding the edges of the paper towel, transfer the quesadilla to a microwave oven.

- Place a second paper towel over the quesadilla and microwave on High for 30 seconds. Check to see if the cheese is melted and the quesadilla is hot. If more cooking is needed, microwave on High for 15-second intervals until the cheese is melted and the tortillas are steamy.

- Remove from the microwave and transfer to a cutting board. Cut the quesadilla into 4 pie-shaped wedges.

MAKES 1 SERVING.

Peanut butter and cookie sandwiches

4   *oatmeal cookies*
About 2 tablespoons peanut butter or Nutella
        (hazelnut spread)
About 2 tablespoons marshmallow creme or chocolate syrup

- Spread the flat side of 2 cookies with the peanut butter and marshmallow creme or chocolate syrup. Place one of the remaining cookies flat-side down on top of each to make a cookie sandwich.

MAKES 1 SERVING.

6 TRICKERY AND TREATS

*H*appiness is death in daytime drama.
It's the Sturm und Drang of our favorite characters' lives
that keeps us watching. Would the John Black/Marlena Evans story
be as poignant if Stefano DiMera weren't determined to keep them apart and
make Marlena his own? Sami Brady Reed is a character we love to hate
for her manipulations of Austin and Carrie Brady Reed. The emotional payoff,
when Carrie learned the truth about Sami and slapped her, was a great
moment in daytime television. Kristen Blake DiMera's cleverness
didn't prevent her downfall; nor will Travis Malloy, Franco Kelly,
or Nurse Lynn be able to avoid the consequences of their treachery.
They may be bad and beautiful, proud and profane, but it's the treacherous
tricksters who make Days of our Lives such a pleasure to watch.

DIVINE DECADENCE

A WOMAN SCONED (SOUR CREAM SCONES)
WITH HONEY CREAM

BROKEN HEART-ICHOKES (BRAISED ARTICHOKES)
AND LINGUINE

BITCHY-SSOISE (CREAMY BASIL POTATO SOUP)

RATTLESNAKE (OR CRABMEAT) IN THE GRASS
(GREEN PASTA)

NOTHING SUCCEEDS LIKE EXCESS

SHRIMP DIAVOLA

STEAKHOUSE STEAK WITH JACK DANIEL'S ONIONS
AND MUSHROOMS

BEING NICE FOR THE HALIBUT

SOLE MATES (SOLE FILLETS BAKED WITH GREEN GRAPES)
WITH RIZ VERTE (GREEN RICE)

WICKED WAYS WITH VEGETABLES

CABBAGE IN CREAM WITH CRISP BACON

CARROTS IN STOLY

POTATOES GRATIN

WILD WILD RICE

SINFULLY SWEET

BRANDIED CHERRY SAUCE
WITH VANITY VANILLA ICE CREAM

MERRY CHOCOLATE MERINGUE
WITH COFFEE CREAM

SMOOTH OPERATOR
WITH HOMEMADE GINGER SNAPS

A TRIFLE EASY WITH CARAMEL SAUCE

A woman sconed (sour cream scones)

2	cups all-purpose flour
2	teaspoons baking powder
1	tablespoon sugar
$^1/_2$	teaspoon salt
$^1/_2$	teaspoon baking soda
4	tablespoons butter
2	eggs, well-beaten
$^1/_2$	cup sour cream
1	tablespoon milk

- Preheat the oven to 425°. Lightly coat a cookie sheet with butter or spray with vegetable cooking spray.

- Combine the flour, baking powder, sugar, salt, and baking soda in a large bowl. Using your fingers or a pastry blender, blend the butter into the flour mixture until the mixture resembles cornmeal.

- Add the eggs, sour cream, and milk; stir until blended. Turn out onto a lightly floured board and knead for about 1 minute. Pat or roll the dough about $^3/_4$-inch thick and cut into rounds using a biscuit cutter or the rim of a water glass about 2 inches in diameter. Place on the prepared cookie sheet and bake for about 15 minutes.

- Serve with Honey Cream (recipe follows) or your favorite jam.

MAKES 8 TO 10 SCONES.

Honey cream

1/4	cup honey
2	tablespoons butter, slightly softened
2	tablespoons sour cream or heavy cream

- Combine the ingredients in a small bowl and beat with electric beaters until fluffy.

MAKES ABOUT 1/2 CUP.

Broken heart–ichokes (braised artichokes)

4	globe artichokes (or 2 8-ounce packages frozen artichokes)
1	lemon
1	cup Italian (or curly) parsley
4	cloves garlic, crushed
1/2	teaspoon crushed red pepper flakes
1	teaspoon salt or to taste
1/2	cup olive oil
2	cups dry white wine, preferably Italian

- Half-fill a large bowl with cold water. Rinse the artichokes. Trim the stems to about 2 inches from the base. Peel the stems to remove the rough exterior. Bend back and snap off the tough outer leaves, one at a time, until only the center with tender, pale green tips remains.

- Using a sharp knife, cut off the tips. Cut the artichoke in half lengthwise. Using a melon baller or small spoon, scrape out and discard the hairy choke.

- Cut each trimmed artichoke half into 4 slices. Place the slices in the cold water. Add the lemon juice and the lemon halves. Repeat with the remaining artichokes, soaking the slices in lemon-water to prevent discoloration.

- Chop the parsley and place in a medium saucepan along with the garlic, red pepper flakes, salt, olive oil, and white wine. Drain the artichoke slices and add to the saucepan.

- Cover the saucepan and place over medium heat, bringing the liquid to a simmer. Lower heat and continue to simmer until the artichokes are very tender, about 45 minutes. Plenty of liquid should remain in the pan.

- Serve warm or at room temperature in soup bowls as an appetizer or side dish, or serve with linguine.

MAKES 4 SERVINGS.

Trickery and Treats

Broken heart–ichokes and linguine

Slices from 4 braised artichokes (see preceding recipe)
1   tablespoon salt or to taste
1   (16-ounce) package linguine

● Keep the artichoke slices warm. Heat a large potful of water to boiling. Add the salt and stir in the linguine. Cook the pasta according to package directions or until tender but still firm to the bite.

● Drain well and return the pasta to the pot. Add the artichokes and all the cooking liquid as sauce.

MAKES 4 SERVINGS.

Bitchy–ssoise (creamy basil potato soup)

$1/2$ stick butter
2   cups chopped onion
2   shallots, finely chopped
2   large russet potatoes, peeled and sliced thickly
4   cups chicken broth
1   bay leaf
1   cup half & half
$1/2$ teaspoon salt or to taste
$1/2$ teaspoon freshly ground pepper or to taste
3 to 4 drops red pepper sauce or to taste (optional)
2   tablespoons shredded fresh basil (or 1 tablespoon dried leaf basil)

● Melt the butter over medium heat in a large saucepan. Add the onion and shallots, and cook until softened, about 5 minutes. Do not

154

brown. Add the potatoes, broth, and bay leaf. Bring the liquid to a boil; reduce heat and simmer until the potatoes are easily pierced with a fork, about 15 minutes. Remove and discard the bay leaf.

- Let the soup cool slightly and then process in batches in a food processor or blender until smooth. Transfer the soup to a container with a tight-fitting lid and cool at room temperature, uncovered. Cover and refrigerate for several hours or overnight until thoroughly chilled.

- Stir the half & half into the chilled soup. Add the salt, pepper, and red pepper sauce to taste. If needed, thin the soup by adding a bit more chicken broth. Top with the shredded basil. (If using dried basil, add to the warm soup after processing.) Serve cold or, if desired, reheat gently and serve warm. Do not allow to boil once the half & half has been added.

MAKES 8 SERVINGS.

KRISTEN BLAKE DiMERA

She started out as such a good, sweet Catholic girl, a social worker at the Horton Center who undeniably loved her "kids." But what woman in her right mind can resist John Black when he turns on the charm? So, despite surrogate dad Stefano DiMera's warnings to stay away, Kris had a tumultuous affair with John—forbidden fruit and all that. With Stefano for a father figure, it's no wonder that Kristen turned out to be a bad seed, although she struggled for years against her baser impulses. But the loyal Kristen resisted allegations that Stefano was an evil man and was heartbroken to learn of his heinous crimes against John and the Bradys. She was equally shocked when husband Tony DiMera turned out to be as wicked as Stefano. A devout Catholic, Kristen encouraged John to explore his assumed identity as a priest, and when the time came, she helped him fight the devil. But surrounded by so much evil, Kristen finally surrendered to its power. First, she lied to Tony; then, she refused to believe John when he denied killing her husband. Kristen also hid John's letter to Marlena Evans, lied about losing her and John's baby, joined with Stefano to fool the man she loved, kidnapped Marlena . . . and the list goes on and on. Kristen is nothing if not determined, so despite the fact that John knows all, she continues to weave her web in hopes of trapping him.

Trickery and Treats

Rattlesnake (or crabmeat) in the grass (green pasta)

The texture of rattlesnake and crab are very similar. Use snake or crabmeat with spinach pasta.

1   *tablespoon plus $1/4$ teaspoon salt or to taste, divided*
8   *ounces spinach fettuccine, linguine or noodles*
$1^1/_2$ *sticks butter*
1   *pound lump crabmeat, picked over to remove any shell (or flaked rattlesnake)*
$^1/_2$ *teaspoon white pepper or to taste*
3   *teaspoons sherry vinegar*

- Preheat the oven broiler. Bring a large potful of water to a boil. Add 1 tablespoon salt and stir in the pasta. Cook according to the package directions until tender but firm to the bite, about 10 minutes. Drain and keep warm.

- In a medium skillet with an ovenproof handle, melt the butter over medium heat. Add the rattlesnake (or crabmeat), salt, and pepper to taste. Cook until creamy white and heated throughout. Sprinkle the sherry vinegar over all and stir. Place the skillet under the oven broiler and broil just until the edges of the rattlesnake (or crabmeat) are golden.

- Pour the butter sauce over the pasta (reserving the snake or crabmeat) and toss to coat well. Arrange on a serving platter (or individual plates) and mound the snake or crabmeat in the middle.

MAKES 4 APPETIZER SERVINGS.

Shrimp diavola

Swimming in butter, these spicy shrimp are indeed an indulgence. You'll want to mop up every drop of sauce with some crusty Italian bread.

2   pounds medium to large shrimp
2   sticks unsalted butter
1   cup red pepper sauce (Tabasco or Louisiana
        hot sauce)
1   tablespoon red pepper flakes
1   tablespoon Worcestershire sauce
Juice from 1 lemon or to taste
2   teaspoons salt or to taste

- Rinse and dry the shrimp but do not peel. Leave the shells and tails on.

- In a large skillet over low heat, combine the butter, red pepper sauce, red pepper flakes, Worcestershire sauce, and lemon juice. Heat until bubbly. Add salt to taste.

- Add the shrimp, stirring to coat. Raise heat to medium and cook, stirring occasionally, just until the shrimp turn pink, about 3 to 5 minutes.

- Serve the shrimp in bowls with lots of sauce and crusty Italian bread for dipping. Provide lots of napkins because these are peel-and-eat shrimp.

MAKES 4 SERVINGS.

NURSE LYNN

Nurse Lynn has a drug problem. It's not cocaine, heroin, or PCP, but it's just as illegal. Her problem started a few years ago when she and another nurse were gossiping about a drug that

could seduce a man into having sex. When candy-striper Sami Brady overheard that juicy tidbit, she broke into the hospital's drug cabinet and slipped her sister's fiancé, Austin Reed, a mickey. Then Sami and Lucas Roberts, her partner in crime, got Lynn a great job out of town to keep her from spilling the beans. When that didn't pan out, Lynn returned to Salem and all was revealed. Lynn should have learned her lesson, but she blew all the cash Kate Roberts gave her for telling the truth. So, Lynn teamed up with Stefano DiMera, who wanted Laura Horton drugged so she wouldn't remember that Stefano and Peter Blake are alive. Nurse Lynn really should practice the medical credo: First, do no harm.

Steakhouse steak with Jack Daniel's onions and mushrooms

A good steak is power food. Don't think you can skimp here. Buy the best cut you can find and spend until it hurts. It'll be worth it.

2	*(12-ounce) porterhouse steaks, 1-inch thick*
1	*tablespoon vegetable oil*
1	*teaspoon salt or to taste*
1	*teaspoon freshly ground black pepper or to taste*
1	*clove garlic, crushed*
2	*tablespoons butter*

- Heat a heavy-bottom skillet, preferably cast iron, over high heat until almost smoking. Remove from heat. Add the oil and swirl to coat the surface of the pan.

- Place the steaks in the pan, one at a time. If the steaks are too large to fit in the pan together, cook them separately.

- Cook on one side until seared and well-crusted, about 5 minutes. Turn, sprinkle the cooked side with salt and pepper to taste, and cook 3 minutes longer for medium-rare (red middle), 4 minutes for medium (light pink middle), or to the desired degree of doneness. Cooking more than medium is not recommended.

- Remove from the skillet and season the other side. Place on a plate that has been warmed in the oven. Set aside.

- With the skillet off heat, add the crushed garlic. Using the back of a spoon, break up the garlic and scrape the bottom of the pan to loosen any crusty bits. Add the butter and stir to melt.

- Pour any juices accumulated from the steaks into the pan and swirl to combine. Pour the butter and pan juices over the steaks and serve with Jack Daniel's Onions and Mushrooms (recipe follows).

MAKES 2 LARGE SERVINGS.

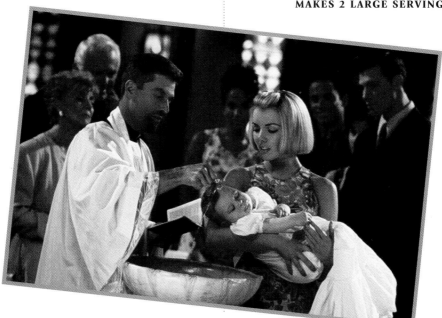

Jack Daniel's onions and mushrooms

3   cups thinly sliced onions
2   cups sliced mushrooms
1   stick butter
3   cloves garlic, crushed
2   tablespoons Jack Daniel's whiskey or bourbon
1   teaspoon salt or to taste
1   teaspoon freshly cracked pepper or to taste

- In a large skillet over medium heat, combine the onions, mushrooms, butter, and garlic. Cook, stirring occasionally, until the onions are soft and golden around the edges. Add the Jack Daniel's whiskey or bourbon and stir. Add salt and pepper to taste. Cook 1 to 2 minutes longer. Serve with Steakhouse Steaks (see preceding recipe).

MAKES 3 TO 4 SERVINGS.

STEFANO DiMERA

His sign is the phoenix, his obsession is Marlena Evans, and he has more lives than a cat. Stefano DiMera, the prince of darkness himself, first came to Salem in 1982, and each subsequent visit has been more nefarious than the previous. He has kidnapped and held prisoner Mickey Horton, Roman Brady, Carrie Brady, Marlena (numerous times), Laura Horton (whose brain he lasered), and John Black (whom he also brainwashed). Stefano killed Curtis Reed and was responsible for Daniel Scott falling out a window to his death as well as the disfigurement and insanity of the Woman In White (Rachel Blake). He provided Kristen Blake with a surrogate mother for her dead baby and is framing Jack Deveraux for Peter Blake's death, even though Peter is still alive. Stefano has survived several explosions, a fall from Marlena's penthouse window, a car crash, being struck by lightning, several heart attacks (mostly faked), and a recurring brain tumor. And, like the Eveready Bunny, he keeps on going . . . and going . . . and going. Stefano doesn't act just to expand his malevolent empire; he is driven by a very strong need to provide for his family. His children include Megan Hathaway and Tony DiMera (both deceased), Benji (who currently lives with his maternal grandfather), Alexandra (Lexie) Carver, and stepkids Peter and Kristen Blake. It was rumored that Renée Dumonde also was Stefano's daughter, but that has not yet been clarified. For such a prolific progenitor, Stefano is a very lonely man, which explains his obsession with Marlena, the woman he sees as the answer to all his prayers.

Trickery and Treats

Being nice for the halibut

4   (6-ounce) halibut steaks (or thick catfish fillets)
1   teaspoon salt or to taste, divided
1   teaspoon freshly cracked pepper or to taste, divided
3/4 cup all-purpose flour
1/2 cup buttermilk
About 1 cup vegetable oil, divided
3   tablespoons unsalted butter
2   tablespoons lime (or lemon) juice
2   tablespoons finely chopped shallots
1/4 cup chopped macadamia nuts or cashews

● Rinse the halibut (or catfish) and pat dry with paper towels. Season the fish with 1/2 teaspoon each salt and pepper. Place the flour and 1/2 teaspoon each salt and pepper in a shallow bowl or on a small plate. Pour the buttermilk into a shallow bowl. Dip the fish into the buttermilk, allowing the excess to drain off. Then dip in the flour, turning to coat all sides. Repeat until all fish pieces are coated. Set aside on waxed paper.

● In a large skillet, place 1/3 inch (about 1 cup) vegetable oil over medium-high heat. When the oil is hot and bubbling at the edges, carefully slide the fish steaks into the oil, 1 at a time. Do not crowd the pan. Cook in batches, adding more oil, if necessary.

● Cook for 2 to 3 minutes on the first side, or until light golden brown. Turn the fish and cook on the other side for 2 to 3 minutes

longer or until golden brown. Reduce heat to medium if the fish browns too fast.

- Remove the skillet from heat and pour off any remaining oil. Wipe out the skillet to clean the surface. Return the skillet to medium-high heat. Add the butter to the skillet and cook until the butter begins to turn light brown. It should smell nutty. Add the lime (or lemon) juice, shallots, and macadamia nuts. Cook for 20 to 30 seconds longer, then drizzle the sauce over the fish.

MAKES 4 SERVINGS.

Sole mates
(sole fillets with green grapes)

1 1/2 *pounds sole fillets*
1   *teaspoon salt or to taste*
1   *teaspoon freshly ground pepper or to taste*

1   *cup seedless green grapes, halved*
1/2 *cup dry white wine*
1   *cup heavy cream*

- Preheat the oven to 450°. Spray a large, shallow baking dish with vegetable cooking spray or coat lightly with butter. The dish should be large enough to hold fillets in a single layer, with edges touching or just overlapping.

- Season the fish with salt and pepper. Arrange the fillets in the baking dish and arrange the green grape halves over the fish. Pour the white wine over all and bake, uncovered, for 12 to 15 minutes. Meanwhile, heat the cream in a small saucepan, but do not boil.

- Remove the baking dish from the oven. Spoon 1/2 cup of the baking liquid into the hot cream, stirring constantly. Pour the cream over the fish. Serve with Riz Verte (recipe follows).

MAKES 4 SERVINGS.

FRANCO KELLY

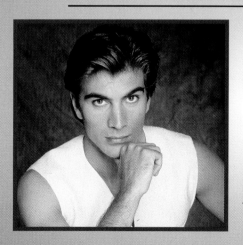

Franco Kelly is 50 percent Italian, 50 percent Irish, and 100 percent Adonis. Kate Roberts lured the gorgeous international model to Salem as a co-conspirator in her plot to break up Bo and Hope Brady, but with unexpected results: Franco fell in love with Hope. That wasn't in the original plan. So, is Franco the bad guy that Bo suspects him to be, or is he the good guy that Billie and Hope know? There's more to our Italian stallion than meets the eye, which Hope discovered in Rome. How bad can Franco be if he still visits and financially supports the nuns at the orphanage where he grew up? Franco is obviously a man of mystery—let's hope his story is as good as John Black's.

Trickery and Treats

Riz verte (green rice)

1   *cup long grain white rice*
2   *cups water*
1   *teaspoon salt*
¹/₂   *stick butter*
¹/₂   *cup finely chopped fresh parsley*

- Place the rice, water, and salt in a saucepan, covered, over high heat or in a microwave-safe cooking dish with the lid on. Bring to a boil over high heat or microwave on High for 5 minutes. Reduce heat to low (or 50 percent power) and cook for 15 minutes or until the liquid is absorbed and the rice is tender.

- Remove from heat or microwave and set aside. Melt the butter in a small skillet and add the parsley. Pour the parsley-butter over the rice and fluff with a fork to combine.

MAKES 4 SERVINGS.

Cabbage in cream with crisp bacon

4   *cups shredded green cabbage (may use packaged shredded cabbage with carrots for slaw)*
1   *stick butter*
¹/₂   *cup chopped onion*
¹/₂   *teaspoon salt or to taste*
1   *teaspoon freshly cracked black pepper or to taste*
¹/₂   *cup heavy cream*
¹/₂   *teaspoon grated nutmeg*
3 to 4 *slices thick-cut bacon, fried crisp and cut into bite-size pieces*

● Place the cabbage in a large pot with enough cold water to cover. Bring the water to a boil and cook for 2 to 3 minutes. Remove from heat and drain the cabbage well; reserve.

● In a large skillet over medium heat, melt the butter and add the onion. Cook until the onion is soft, about 3 to 5 minutes. Add the well-drained cabbage and stir to coat with butter. Add the salt and pepper. Pour the cream over the cabbage and stir in the nutmeg. Cover and simmer over low heat for about 5 minutes to meld the flavors.

● Sprinkle with crisp bacon just before serving.

MAKES 4 TO 6 SERVINGS.

Carrots in Stoly

1   (8-ounce) package peeled baby carrots
$^1/_2$ cup Stolichnaya (or other vodka)
1   tablespoon finely grated orange peel
        (orange part only)
1   teaspoon sugar
$^1/_2$ teaspoon salt or to taste
$^1/_2$ teaspoon freshly cracked pepper or to taste

● Place the carrots, vodka, orange peel, sugar, salt, and pepper in a medium saucepan over medium heat.

● Bring to a boil; immediately reduce heat to low and simmer until carrots are tender, about 10 minutes. Adjust seasoning to taste with sugar, salt, and pepper.

MAKES 4 SERVINGS.

Potatoes gratin

4   (1$^1/_2$ pounds) russet potatoes
1   tablespoon butter, melted
2   eggs, lightly beaten
1   cup milk or half & half
$^1/_2$ teaspoon grated nutmeg
1   teaspoon salt or to taste
1   teaspoon freshly ground black pepper or to taste
1   cup grated Gruyère (Swiss) cheese

● Preheat the oven to 300°. Spray a 9x11-inch baking pan or similar-size baking dish with vegetable cooking spray.

● Peel the potatoes and slice $^1/_4$-inch thick. Place a single layer of potatoes in the pan. Combine the melted butter, eggs, milk, nutmeg, salt, and pepper.

● Cover the potatoes with one-fourth of the milk mixture. Continue layering until all ingredients are used up, ending with cheese on top.

● Cover the pan loosely with foil and bake for 45 to 50 minutes or until the potatoes are tender. Remove the foil and increase the oven temperature to 425°. Return to the oven until the potatoes are brown, about 5 to 10 minutes.

MAKES 6 SERVINGS.

Wild wild rice

$1/2$	stick butter
$1/2$	cup chopped onion
$1/2$	cup chopped celery
$1/2$	cup sliced (or chopped) fresh shiitake mushrooms
$1/4$	cup dried cherries
1	teaspoon dried thyme
$1/2$	cup wild rice
$1/2$	cup long-grain brown rice
$1/2$	cup long-grain white rice
3	cups hot chicken broth
1	teaspoon salt or to taste
1	teaspoon freshly cracked black pepper or to taste
$1/2$	cup chopped parsley

● In a large saucepan, melt the butter over medium heat. Add the onion, celery, mushrooms, dried cherries, and thyme. Cook until the onion is softened but not brown, 3 to 5 minutes.

● Add the rices and stir to coat the grains. Add the hot chicken broth, salt, and pepper. Bring the liquid to a boil over high heat. Reduce heat and simmer for 30 minutes or until most of the moisture is absorbed and the rices are tender. Add a bit more liquid (water or broth) and cook for 5 to 10 minutes longer, if needed, to soften the rices.

● Stir in the parsley and adjust seasoning to taste.

● To use as a dressing for roast pork or roast turkey, place the cooked rice mixture in a shallow baking dish sprayed with vegetable cooking spray. Cover with foil and bake in the oven along with the roast during the last 30 to 45 minutes of cooking time.

MAKES 4 TO 5 SERVINGS.

TRAVIS MALLOY

It's not really clear whether he's Travis Malloy or Trent Davis. What is clear is that he's working for Stefano DiMera. Also unclear is why—or whether—Stefano has his usual diabolical hold over him. Travis seems to be more of a loose cannon than most of the DiMera minions. Jack Deveraux met Travis while in jail. Travis supposedly was transferred to another prison, but when attorney Mickey Horton tried to trace him, there was no record of his incarceration. Now, Travis is living next door to Jennifer Blake and is using the name Trent. While Jack's away, Travis may play, but Jack won't be in prison forever. That's when Travis/Trent's true identity— and deeds—will likely be revealed.

Brandied cherry sauce with vanity vanilla ice cream

2 cups (1 12-ounce bag) frozen dark sweet cherries, unsweetened
1/4 cup sugar
About 1/4 cup cognac or brandy
2 teaspoons cornstarch dissolved in 2 teaspoons water

● Thaw the cherries in the refrigerator or in the microwave on Low power until just slightly softened. Place a colander over a bowl and pour the cherries into the colander. Allow to defrost completely, catching the juices as they drain, about 20 to 30 minutes.

● Add enough water to the drained cherry juice to equal 1 cup. Empty the cherry liquid into a medium saucepan. Add the sugar and bring the mixture to a boil over high heat, stirring constantly. Add the cherries and the cognac or brandy. Reduce heat and simmer for 1 minute. Stir in the dissolved cornstarch and cook just until bubbly and thickened, 2 to 3 minutes longer.

● Serve warm over Vanity Vanilla Ice Cream (recipe follows) or store-bought.

MAKES 6 SERVINGS.

Vanity vanilla ice cream

$1/2$	cup sugar
4	egg yolks
2	cups hot milk
2	cups heavy cream
$1/4$	teaspoon salt
1	tablespoon vanilla extract

● Combine the sugar and egg yolks in a large saucepan. Beat until thick using a wire whisk or electric beaters. Very slowly, and beating constantly so as not to hard-cook the eggs, add the hot milk. Simmer over low heat until slightly thickened.

● Remove from heat and strain, if desired, into a large pitcher or other container. Allow to cool completely in the refrigerator.

● Add the cream, salt, and vanilla. Place in the freezer container of an ice cream freezer. Freeze according to manufacturer's directions.

MAKES 6 SERVINGS (ABOUT 3 PINTS).

Merry chocolate meringue with coffee cream

4	egg whites, at room temperature
$1/2$	teaspoon cream of tartar
$1/2$	teaspoon vanilla extract
1	cup sugar, divided
$1/4$	cup cocoa
Pinch of salt	
$1/2$	cup finely chopped pecans

● Preheat the oven to 250°. Lightly butter an 8x8-inch or 9x9-inch pie pan.

● Place the egg whites, cream of tartar, and vanilla in a medium bowl. Using an electric mixer,

beat until soft peaks form, gradually adding $1/2$ cup sugar while beating.

● In a small bowl, mix the remaining $1/2$ cup sugar with the cocoa and salt. Gradually add the sugar-cocoa mixture to the first bowl, beating constantly until stiff peaks form. Using a rubber spatula, carefully fold the pecans into the meringue. Place in the prepared cake pan.

● Bake for 45 minutes or until the meringue is dry on the outside and lightly browned. Remove from the oven and cool completely. Carefully remove the meringue from the cake pan and place on a serving plate. Cover with Coffee Cream (recipe follows).

MAKES 8 SERVINGS.

Coffee cream

1	cup heavy cream, well-chilled
$1/4$	cup sugar
1	teaspoon cocoa
$1/2$	teaspoon powdered instant coffee or espresso

● Beat the cream until peaks start to form. Combine the sugar, cocoa, and instant coffee in a small bowl. Gradually add to the cream, beating constantly until stiff peaks form.

● Spread over the cooled meringue or use to garnish an angel food cake.

MAKES 2 CUPS OR 8 SERVINGS.

Smooth operator with homemade ginger snaps

¹/₂ cup brandy
¹/₂ cup white crème de cacao
About 2 cups slightly softened Vanity Vanilla Ice Cream
  (see preceding recipe) or store-bought
¹/₂ teaspoon grated nutmeg
2 to 4 ice cubes

● Combine all the ingredients in a blender container. Blend just until the consistency of a milk shake. Pour into chilled tumblers and serve with Homemade Ginger Snaps (recipe follows) or store-bought.

MAKES 4 SERVINGS.

Homemade ginger snaps

³/₄ cup vegetable shortening
2 cups sugar, divided
1 egg
2 cups all-purpose flour
2 teaspoons baking soda
¹/₂ teaspoon salt
1 tablespoon ground ginger
1 teaspoon allspice
¹/₄ cup molasses

● Preheat the oven to 350°. Lightly spray 2 to 3 cookie sheets with vegetable cooking spray.

● In a large bowl, using an electric mixer, beat together the shortening and 1 cup sugar until smooth. Add the egg and beat until light and fluffy.

● In a medium bowl, stir together the flour, baking soda, salt, ginger, and allspice. Add to the shortening mixture, along with the molasses, beating until smooth and well-blended.

● Roll the dough into 1-inch balls. Roll each ball in the remaining 1 cup sugar. Place about 2 inches apart on the prepared cookie sheets and bake for 10 to 12 minutes or until the cookies have spread and the tops have cracked. Remove the cookies and place on racks to cool.

MAKES ABOUT 40 COOKIES.

A trifle easy with homemade caramel sauce

3   cups bakery pound cake (about 1 cake), cut into
     1-inch cubes
2   cups sliced strawberries, peaches, or bananas
1/2 cup sherry or dark rum
1   (3.4-ounce) package instant vanilla pudding mix
2   cups cold milk
1   cup heavy cream, well-chilled
1   cup bakery macaroon cookies, crumbled (optional)

- In a glass serving bowl with steep sides, toss together the pound cake and sliced fruit. Sprinkle the sherry or rum over the cake and fruit, tossing to coat well.

- In a medium mixing bowl, combine the vanilla pudding mix and cold milk. Beat with electric beaters on low speed until slightly thickened, about 1 to 2 minutes. Pour the pudding over the cake and fruit, spreading to the edges of the dish to seal. Scrape the sides as clean as possible with a rubber spatula.

- Place the cream in the mixing bowl. Using electric beaters on high speed, beat until stiff peaks form. Spoon the whipped cream on top, spreading to the edges of the bowl. Sprinkle with crumbled macaroons, if desired. Cover and refrigerate for at least 1 hour or until well chilled. Serve with Homemade Caramel Sauce (recipe follows), if desired.

MAKES 8 TO 10 SERVINGS.

Homemade caramel sauce

1/3 pound caramels
3/4 cup evaporated milk (not sweetened
     condensed milk)

- Unwrap the caramels and place in a double-boiler over—not in—boiling water. Add the evaporated milk. Cook, stirring frequently, until the caramels are melted and the sauce is smooth.

- *Shortcut:* Place the caramels and milk in a microwave-safe 2-cup glass measure. Microwave on High for 30 seconds at a time, stirring after each interval, until the caramels are melted and the sauce is smooth.

MAKES ABOUT 1 CUP.

7 DAYS OF OUR LIVES
ON THE SET

*P*utting together a television series as technically complex as Days of our Lives is no easy feat. One of the things that gives the show its sense of movement is that each episode contains over thirty scenes, more than most other daytime dramas. To make those scenes more interesting, Days' writers utilize as many different sets as the sound stages can accommodate. The taping of scenes that involve a large number of cast members and extras, such as weddings or parties, can run well into the wee hours of the next morning. When the producers know that a long and complicated day of shooting lies ahead, they usually hire Los Angeles area catering firm Jennie Cook's to provide the evening meal. The cast and crew all agree the food is exceptional, and Jenny never brings the same selections twice, unless requested. And the requests fairly pour in. So, any time you see a scene with a large number of characters—such as Carrie and Austin's wedding, the Marie Antoinette Ball, or any holiday celebration—it's virtually certain that the cast enjoyed a sumptuous spread from Jennie Cook's on the night that episode was taped.

Days of our Lives *On the Set*

M E N U   O N E

MIXED GREENS WITH DRIED PEACHES,
WALNUTS, FETA AND
MISS LEMON'S VINAIGRETTE

GREEN BEANS WITH CHILI PECANS
AND SESAME DRESSING

LEMON ARTICHOKE CHICKEN

POTATOES TIAN

ALFREDO SAUCE

EASY FRUIT CRUNCH

FUDGE BROWNIES

Mixed greens with dried peaches, walnuts, and feta

2   (12-ounce) bags salad blend, preferably mesclun
1/2   cup dried peaches, cut into thin strips
1/2   cup crumbled feta cheese
1/2   cup Toasted Walnut Pieces (recipe follows)
Miss Lemon's Vinaigrette (recipe follows)
1   teaspoon salt or to taste
1   teaspoon freshly cracked pepper or to taste

- In a large salad bowl, toss together the salad blend, dried peach strips, feta cheese, and walnut pieces. Pour about 1/2 cup vinaigrette over the salad and toss to coat well. Add additional dressing, if desired. Season to taste with salt and pepper. Toss again and serve. Store the remaining dressing in the refrigerator.

MAKES 8 SERVINGS.

Toasted walnut pieces

1/2   cup walnut pieces
Nonstick vegetable spray

- Pick over the walnuts to remove any shell. Chop the walnut pieces to a uniform size.

- Lightly spray the bottom of a small skillet with vegetable cooking spray and place over medium heat. Add the walnuts and cook, stirring frequently, until the walnuts just begin to turn golden. Remove from heat and turn the walnuts out of the pan to stop cooking.

MAKES 1/2 CUP.

Miss Lemon's Vinaigrette

1/3   cup lemon juice
2   teaspoons sugar
1   teaspoon Dijon mustard
1   cup corn oil
1/2   teaspoon salt or to taste
Pinch of cayenne pepper or to taste

- In a medium bowl (or jar with a tight-fitting lid), combine the lemon juice, sugar, and mustard. Stir with a wire whisk (or secure lid and shake well) until the sugar is dissolved.

- Whisking constantly, add the oil slowly until the mixture is thickened and cloudy. (Or add the oil to the jar, secure the lid and shake until the mixture is thickened and cloudy.) Store in the refrigerator.

MAKES 1 1/3 CUPS.

Green beans with chili pecans and sesame dressing

1 (16-ounce) package frozen green beans (uncut)
1   teaspoon salt or to taste
2 to 3 teaspoons sugar or to taste
Chili Pecans (recipe follows)
Sesame Dressing (recipe follows)

● Bring a large potful of water to a boil over high heat. Add the green beans, salt, and sugar, stirring to separate the pieces. When the water returns to a boil, cook for 2 to 4 minutes and drain the beans. Rinse with cold water to stop cooking.

● Allow the beans to cool to room temperature. Sprinkle the Chili Pecans over the beans. Pour ¹/₂ cup Sesame Dressing over the beans and toss well. Add more dressing as needed.

MAKES 6 SERVINGS.

Days of our Lives *On the Set*

Chili pecans

1   cup pecan pieces
2   tablespoons brown sugar
$^1/_2$ teaspoon cayenne pepper or to taste
2 to 3 tablespoons water
Pinch of salt or to taste

● Preheat the oven to 350˚.

● In a small bowl, combine the pecan pieces, brown sugar, cayenne pepper, 2 tablespoons water, and salt. Mix well to coat the pecans evenly. Add a bit more water, if needed, to dissolve the brown sugar.

● Spray a jelly roll pan or cookie sheet with vegetable cooking spray and spread the pecans in a single layer. Place in the oven and bake for 8 to 10 minutes or until the pecans are golden and toasty. Watch carefully; nuts burn easily. Remove from the oven and allow to cool. Store the nuts in an airtight container.

MAKES 1 CUP.

Sesame dressing

2   tablespoons Chinese sesame oil
$^1/_2$ cup vegetable oil
$^1/_2$ cup rice or cider vinegar
1   tablespoon soy sauce
$^1/_3$ cup sugar
1   teaspoon Dijon mustard
1   teaspoon lemon juice
1   clove garlic, finely chopped
$^1/_2$ teaspoon grated fresh ginger

● Combine the sesame oil and vegetable oil in a pourable measure. In a medium bowl, stir together the vinegar, soy sauce, sugar, mustard, lemon juice, garlic, and ginger, using a wire whisk. Stirring constantly, slowly add the oils. (Or combine all ingredients in a jar with a tight-fitting lid and shake to combine the ingredients.)

● Shake or mix the dressing well before each use as the dressing will separate after sitting. Refrigerate any leftovers.

MAKES ABOUT 1$^2/_3$ CUPS.

Lemon artichoke chicken

4   *skinless, boneless chicken breast halves*
$1/3$ *cup instant-dissolving (Wondra) flour*
$1/4$ *teaspoon salt or to taste*
$1/8$ *teaspoon pepper or to taste*
1   *cup vegetable oil or as needed*
2   *teaspoons finely chopped fresh garlic*
1   *(6-ounce) jar marinated artichokes, drained*
1   *cup chicken stock*
1   *tablespoon capers, drained (optional)*
Juice of $1/2$ lemon
Thin slices fresh lemon for garnish (optional)

- Preheat the oven to 300˚. Rinse and dry the chicken breast halves. In a shallow bowl, combine the flour, salt, and pepper, mixing well.

- Dip the chicken into the flour mixture, turning to coat all sides. Set aside on waxed paper.

- Meanwhile, pour the oil into a large skillet to a depth of about $1/2$ inch. Heat over medium-high heat. When the oil is hot, add the chicken pieces, 2 to 3 at a time. Cook until golden on one side; turn and cook until brown on the other side. Drain on paper towels and arrange the chicken pieces in a shallow baking pan. Cover and place in the oven to keep warm.

- Pour off all but about 1 tablespoon oil. Add the garlic and cook over medium heat for 2 to 3 minutes. Add the artichokes. Stir occasionally and cook until the artichokes are light brown around the edges.

- Add the chicken stock and capers, if desired. Raise heat to high and cook until the stock is reduced by about half. Pour the sauce and artichokes over the chicken. Drizzle with lemon juice. Garnish with lemon slices, if desired.

MAKES 4 SERVINGS.

Potatoes Tian

4   large (about 2 pounds) russet potatoes
Nonstick vegetable spray
1   teaspoon salt or to taste
1   teaspoon freshly cracked pepper or to taste
2   (8-ounce) packages frozen chopped spinach, thawed
         and well-drained
2   cups chopped tomatoes, drained (may use canned
         or fresh)
16   ounces mozzarella cheese, shredded
4   cups Alfredo sauce (recipe follows) or substitute
         bottled sauce
$^1/_2$ cup shredded fresh Parmesan cheese

- Preheat the oven to 350°. Spray a large baking sheet and a 9x13-inch baking dish with nonstick vegetable spray.

- Peel and slice the potatoes into $^1/_4$-inch-thick rounds. Arrange the potatoes in a single layer on the prepared baking sheet. Spray the tops of the potatoes with nonstick vegetable spray and season generously with salt and pepper.

- Bake for 25 minutes or until the potatoes are tender and easily pierced with a fork. Remove the potatoes from the oven and loosen with a spatula; reserve.

- Spoon just enough Alfredo sauce into the prepared 9x13-inch baking dish to cover the bottom. Top with a single layer of roasted potatoes, overlapping the edges if necessary, to cover the sauce.

- Make sure the spinach is well-drained. Place the spinach in a colander and press out the excess liquid using the back of a spoon. Dot tablespoonfuls of drained spinach evenly over the potatoes. Sprinkle with the chopped tomatoes. Add a generous layer of mozzarella cheese. Spoon Alfredo sauce over all in an even layer to the edges of the pan.

- Add another layer of roasted potatoes, pressing down to allow room for the remaining ingredients. Dot with the reserved spinach and sprinkle with the reserved tomatoes and mozzarella cheese. Cover with Alfredo sauce.

- Arrange a few potatoes on top for garnish and sprinkle with Parmesan cheese. Place the baking dish in the oven over a cookie sheet or foil on the rack underneath to catch any drips. Bake until bubbly and golden, about 30 minutes. Cool for 15 minutes before serving.

MAKES 8 SERVINGS.

Alfredo sauce

2   (8-ounce) packages cream cheese, softened to
      room temperature
2   eggs, lightly beaten (may use $^{1}/_{2}$ cup pasteurized
      egg substitute, such as Egg Beaters, to eliminate
      concerns about raw eggs)
$^{2}/_{3}$ cup grated fresh Parmesan cheese
$^{1}/_{4}$ teaspoon grated fresh pepper or to taste
$^{1}/_{4}$ to $^{1}/_{3}$ cup milk, as needed

- Place the cream cheese in a medium mixing
  bowl and beat, using electric beaters on
  medium speed, until almost smooth.

- Add the eggs and continue beating, adding the
  Parmesan cheese and pepper.

- When all ingredients are well-incorporated and
  smooth, stir the mixture into hot, drained
  pasta noodles, traditionally fettuccine.

MAKES ABOUT 4 CUPS.

*Note: If using with Potatoes Tian (see preceding
recipe), add the milk as necessary to create a smooth
spreading consistency.*

Easy fruit crunch

4   cups fresh or frozen blackberries, blueberries, or
     boysenberries
1¼ cups all-purpose flour, divided
1¼ plus ⅓ cups sugar, divided
1   teaspoon salt, divided
1   egg
1   teaspoon vanilla extract
1   tablespoon vegetable oil
½   cup quick-cooking oats
¾   cup firmly packed brown sugar
1   teaspoon cinnamon
1   teaspoon baking powder
2 to 4 tablespoons butter, melted (optional)

● Preheat the oven to 350°. Spray a 9x13-inch baking dish with vegetable cooking spray.

● In a medium bowl, toss together the berries, ¼ cup flour, 1¼ cups sugar, and ½ teaspoon salt. Spread the berries evenly in the bottom of the prepared baking dish.

● In the same bowl, beat together the egg, vanilla, and vegetable oil. In another small bowl, combine 1 cup flour, the oats, brown sugar, ⅓ cup sugar, cinnamon, baking powder, and ½ teaspoon salt.

● Add the dry ingredients to the beaten egg, fluffing with a fork until crumbly. Arrange the crust mixture evenly over the berries. Drizzle with the melted butter, if desired. Place in the oven and bake for 35 minutes, until bubbly and the crust is golden.

MAKES 10 SERVINGS.

Fudge brownies

2   sticks butter
½   cup unsweetened cocoa
2   cups sugar
1   tablespoon vanilla extract
4   eggs, lightly beaten
1   cup all-purpose flour
1   cup chopped pecans or walnuts (optional)
Confectioners' sugar (optional)

● Preheat the oven to 350°. Grease and flour a 9x13-inch pan.

● Place the butter in a large saucepan over low heat to melt. When the butter is melted, add the cocoa, sugar, and vanilla, stirring to blend well. Remove from heat and allow to cool slightly.

● Stir in the eggs and flour, mixing just until blended. Add the nuts and stir to blend. Pour the batter into the prepared pan. Bake for 25 to 30 minutes or until the brownies pull away from the sides of the pan.

● Remove from the oven and allow to cool completely before cutting into squares. Dust the squares with confectioners' sugar, if desired.

MAKES ABOUT 24 SERVINGS.

M E N U   T W O

TOMATO BISQUE

WATERCRESS AND SPINACH SALAD

ATLANTIC SALMON PINARI

FUDGE PIE

Tomato bisque

3 *tablespoons vegetable oil*
$^1/_2$ *cup chopped onion*
$^1/_4$ *cup instant-dissolving (Wondra) flour*
4 *cups milk*
1 *bay leaf (optional)*
$^1/_2$ *teaspoon baking soda*
2 *cups tomato sauce*
1 *cup canned tomatoes, drained*
1 to 2 *teaspoons sugar or to taste*
1 *teaspoon salt or to taste*
1 *teaspoon white pepper or to taste*

● In a large saucepan over medium heat, add the oil and onion. Cook until the onion is golden. Stir the flour into the onion and cook for about 2 minutes.

● Slowly add the milk, stirring constantly with a wire whisk. Add the bay leaf, if desired. Cook until thickened slightly, about 5 to 10 minutes.

● Stir the baking soda into the tomato sauce. This will stabilize the acid so the milk won't curdle. Stir the tomato sauce into the milk mixture. Heat throughout and strain through a sieve or fine-mesh colander.

● Chop the tomatoes and add to the soup. Heat throughout. Add sugar and salt and pepper to taste.

MAKES 6 SERVINGS.

Watercress and spinach salad with strawberries

To make a double batch, follow the directions in parentheses.

1   (2) bunch(es) watercress
2   (4) bunches spinach
¹/₂ (1) pint strawberries
2   (3) cups enoki mushrooms
2   (4) tablespoons balsamic vinegar
¹/₂ (1) cup honey
³/₄ (1¹/₂) cup(s) vegetable or olive oil
1   (2) teaspoon(s) salt or to taste
1   (2) teaspoon(s) freshly cracked black pepper or to taste

● Combine the watercress and spinach in a sinkful of cold water. Dunk the leaves several times and drain. Repeat the procedure twice. After the third rinsing, do not drain the sink. Instead, lift the leaves out of the water and place them in a large colander, shaking off as much water as possible. Allow leaves to drain.

● Place the leaves on several layers of paper towels. Add several layers of towels on top. Allow to drain, turning several times so the layers of towels can absorb as much liquid as possible.

● Meanwhile, rinse and dry the strawberries. Select several pretty, large berries and reserve for garnish. Remove the stems from the remaining strawberries and cut the berries in half; reserve.

● Slice off the bottoms of the mushrooms and reserve.

● In a large salad bowl, combine the vinegar, honey, oil, salt, and pepper. Stir or whisk together until well-blended.

● When the watercress and spinach leaves are dry, discard the towels. Tear off the stems (tear large leaves into bite-size pieces) and drop the leaves into the salad bowl. Add the strawberries and mushrooms. Toss to combine and evenly coat the ingredients with salad dressing.

● Adjust seasoning with salt and pepper, if desired. Arrange whole strawberries on top of the salad.

MAKES 4 (8) SERVINGS.

Atlantic salmon Pinari

This was developed for Dr. Peace, who insisted on non-fat recipes way back in 1984. Sacrificing taste was never an option.

8   (4-ounce) salmon fillets
1¹/₂ cups pineapple juice, divided
2   tablespoons soy sauce, divided
1   teaspoon finely chopped or grated ginger, divided
1   teaspoon cornstarch
2   teaspoons sugar or honey
1   tablespoon sesame seeds for garnish
¹/₂ cup thinly sliced green onion (green and white parts)
4   cups boiled white rice, if desired

● Rinse and dry the salmon fillets. Place the fillets in a resealable plastic bag.

● Pour ³/₄ cup pineapple juice, 1 tablespoon soy sauce, and ³/₄ teaspoon ginger into the bag. Marinate for about 20 to 30 minutes.

● Preheat the oven broiler.

● Remove the fillets from the marinade, shaking off any excess. Discard the marinade. Place the fillets, skin-side down, in a single layer in a broiler pan. Place under a hot broiler, 4 to 5 inches from the heat. Broil for 4 to 6 minutes or until an instant meat thermometer registers 120° to 130°. Do not turn. Keep warm.

- In a small saucepan, combine ³/₄ cup pineapple juice and the cornstarch, stirring to dissolve the cornstarch. Add 1 tablespoon soy sauce, ¹/₄ teaspoon minced ginger, and the sugar. Place over medium heat and cook, stirring constantly, until thickened. Remove from heat.

- Pour the sauce over the salmon. Sprinkle with the sesame seeds and green onion. Serve with boiled white rice, if desired.

- *Variation:* Grate 1 fresh pineapple, to make about 1¹/₂ cups. Add 1 tablespoon soy sauce and 1 to 2 teaspoons maple syrup or sugar (optional); reserve. Preheat the oven broiler. In a small bowl, combine 2 tablespoons soy sauce, 2 teaspoons sugar, and ¹/₄ cup vegetable

oil. Place the salmon fillets in a single layer in a broiler pan. Brush the soy sauce mixture over the salmon. Broil for 3 to 5 minutes. Remove the broiler pan from the oven and gently spoon an even layer of the pineapple mixture on top of each fillet. Gently press the pineapple into the salmon to create a smooth, even layer. Return to the oven and broil for 2 to 3 minutes longer, or until the pineapple crust is a light, golden brown. Prepare the glaze; garnish and serve as above.

MAKES 8 SERVINGS.

Fudge pie

1	*cup sugar*
3	*eggs, lightly beaten*
¹/₂	*cup corn syrup*
¹/₂	*cup cocoa*
¹/₂	*stick butter, melted and cooled*
2	*teaspoons vanilla extract*
¹/₄	*teaspoon salt*
¹/₂	*cup semisweet chocolate chips*

1 unbaked (9-inch) pie shell (see Simple Pastry recipe on page 58) or use a prepared pie shell
Whipped cream for garnish

- Preheat the oven to 325°. Combine the sugar, eggs, corn syrup, cocoa, butter, vanilla, and salt. Stir until smooth. Pour the filling into the pie shell. Sprinkle the chocolate chips in an even layer over the filling.

- Place in the oven and bake for 45 to 50 minutes or until the filling is set and the center no longer appears loose and liquid. Serve warm with whipped cream.

MAKES 8 SERVINGS.

MENU THREE

CHICKEN PIECES WITH MIRIAM'S MARINADE

BASMATI PILAF SALAD
WITH BALSAMIC VINAIGRETTE

ROASTED CARROTS

ALLISON'S CHUNK CHOCOLATE CHIP COOKIES

DR. BIRD BANANA CAKE

Chicken pieces with Miriam's marinade

Once upon a time, a cook named Miriam worked in Jennie's catering kitchen. She fell in love with the salad chef. They ran away together and lived happily ever after. All that is left is Miriam's Marinade, which is spectacular on pieces of bone-in chicken. It's great, even for breakfast, on the rare occasion that any chicken is left over.

1	whole chicken, cut into serving pieces, or 8 pieces of bone-in chicken, such as thighs, drumsticks, or breast halves (or a combination)
$1/2$	cup honey
$1/2$	cup soy sauce
4	tablespoons chopped fresh basil (leaves from about 5 stalks)
$1/2$	cup red wine
1	tablespoon lemon juice

- Rinse and dry the chicken pieces and place in a resealable plastic bag.

- In a small bowl, stir together the honey, soy sauce, basil, red wine, and lemon juice until well-blended. Pour over the chicken pieces and place in the refrigerator overnight, turning several times.

- Preheat the oven to 350°. Line a baking pan with aluminum foil. Drain the chicken pieces and discard the marinade. Place the chicken in a single layer in the prepared baking pan. Bake for 45 minutes to 1 hour or until the juices run clear when the chicken is pierced with a fork. If cooking light and dark meat at the same time, test for doneness of the thighs or drumsticks since dark meat takes a bit longer to cook.

- If desired, the chicken may be grilled over low coals. Reserve some marinade for basting. Proceed as above.

MAKES 4 SERVINGS.

Basmati pilaf salad

Although regular white rice may be used for this salad, basmati rice, which is available in ethnic markets and specialty sections of some large supermarkets, is preferred. This highly fragrant Indian rice cooks up with a soft texture and takes on the flavor of stock and vegetables more readily than does plain white rice.

6	cups strong vegetarian (or chicken) stock
3	cups coarsely chopped carrots
3	cups basmati rice
1	cup crumbled feta cheese
2	cups coarsely chopped fresh tomatoes
3	cups coarsely shredded or chopped spinach, lightly packed
1	cup toasted walnuts
1	cup currants
2	cups Balsamic Vinaigrette (recipe follows) or to taste

- In a large saucepan over high heat, combine the stock, carrots, and rice. Bring the liquid to a boil. Reduce heat to low; cover and cook until the rice is tender and the liquid is absorbed, about 20 minutes.

- Allow the rice to cool completely before adding other ingredients.

- When the rice is completely cooled, turn the rice into a large salad bowl. Fluff with a fork to separate the grains. Add the feta cheese, tomatoes, spinach, walnuts, and currants. Toss to distribute the ingredients evenly. Pour the Balsamic Vinaigrette over the salad and toss again to coat the ingredients.

MAKES 8 SERVINGS.

Balsamic vinaigrette

1   tablespoon Dijon mustard
1   teaspoon dried Italian herb blend (or $^1/_2$ teaspoon
        each dried leaf basil and leaf oregano)
$^1/_3$ cup balsamic vinegar
1   wedge of red onion, about the size and thickness of a
        deck of cards
1   cup apple cider vinegar
2   cups corn oil
1   teaspoon salt or to taste
1   teaspoon freshly cracked pepper or to taste

- In a blender, combine the mustard, herbs, balsamic vinegar, and onion. If necessary, cut the onion into several pieces for easier blending. On high speed or puree, blend the ingredients until finely chopped. Turn the blender off several times while chopping and stir down the ingredients. Process until smooth like fine applesauce.

- With the blender running on low speed, pour in the corn oil, adding in a slow, steady stream.

Taste and check consistency. It should be like a thick salad dressing. With the blender running, add a bit more oil, if desired.

- Add salt and pepper to taste. Store in the refrigerator for several weeks.

MAKES ABOUT 4 CUPS.

Jennie's roasted carrots

Jennie Cook's signature carrot recipe!

1   tablespoon achiote paste* dissolved in 1 tablespoon
        water or 1 tablespoon chili powder
2   tablespoons olive oil
$^1/_2$ to 1 tablespoons white sugar
$^1/_2$ cup water
1 or 2 bunch(es) small carrots, scrubbed clean with ends
        trimmed but unpeeled.

- Preheat the oven to 400°. Combine the achiote paste or chili powder, olive oil, sugar, and water. Stir to blend well.

- Line a jelly roll pan or other shallow-sided baking pan with oil. Arrange the carrots in a single layer. Pour the blended seasoning evenly over the carrots. Place in the oven and bake for about 45 minutes or until the carrots are shriveled and toasty brown.

- Pour the pan juices over the carrots and serve.

MAKES 4 TO 6 SERVINGS.
Achiote paste is a South American spice blend. It comes in a brick or a paste. If it is not available, substitute chili powder.

Allison's chunk chocolate chip cookies

To Jennie's surprise, her urban daughter became a member of the 4-H Club. This delicious recipe was created for her 4-H Fair. The cookies are chewy on the inside and crispy on the edges. Unless you like perfectly shaped cookies, you don't have to roll them into small balls, just drop them by the spoonful.

2   sticks butter, softened to room temperature
1   cup firmly packed brown sugar
1/2 cup sugar
1   teaspoon vanilla extract
2   eggs
2 1/2 cups all-purpose flour
1/2 teaspoon baking soda
1/4 teaspoon salt
1   cup semisweet baking chocolate, cut into
        pea-size chunks
1   cup semi-sweet chocolate chips

● Preheat the oven to 350°. Spray large cookie sheets with nonstick cooking spray.

● In a large bowl, beat together the butter, brown sugar, sugar, and vanilla until light and fluffy using electric beaters on high speed. Add the eggs one at a time, blending on medium speed after each addition.

● In a medium bowl, sift together the flour, baking soda, and salt. Stir the dry ingredients into the butter mixture, blending with a wooden spoon or spatula. Do not overmix. Stir in the chocolate chunks and chips.

● Roll the dough into small balls, about the size of a cherry tomato, and place on the prepared cookie sheets about 2 inches apart or drop by the tablespoonful. Bake for 8 to 10 minutes or until the edges are golden.

MAKES 4 TO 4 1/2 DOZEN COOKIES.

Dr. Bird banana cake

Dr. Bird is a mythical person who haunts the kitchens of Sellersville, Pennsylvania, where Jennie grew up. Everyone in town has this recipe, but no one knows where it came from. This easy recipe makes a very rich banana cake and is well worth the wait for ripe bananas.

3   cups all-purpose flour
1   teaspoon baking soda
1   teaspoon cinnamon
1   teaspoon salt
2   cups sugar
1 1/2 cups vegetable oil
1   (8-ounce) can crushed pineapple, undrained
1 1/2 teaspoons vanilla extract
3   eggs, lightly beaten
2   cups chopped or mashed ripe bananas
1   cup nuts, chopped
Confectioners' sugar for garnish

● Preheat the oven to 325°. Grease and flour a Bundt pan.

● In a large bowl, combine the flour, baking soda, cinnamon, salt, sugar, oil, undrained pineapple, vanilla, eggs, bananas, and nuts. Using a wooden spoon or spatula, mix until the ingredients are moistened and the batter is well-combined.

● Pour into the prepared Bundt pan. Place in the oven and bake for 1 hour and 20 minutes or until the top is brown and crusty. Remove from the oven and allow to cool on a rack for about 10 minutes. Invert the cake on the rack and cool completely.

● Lift off the Bundt pan. Transfer the cake to a serving platter. Sift confectioners' sugar over the top.

MAKES 12 TO 16 SERVINGS.

Index

Index

Index

Index

Index